JESUS

and the

JIHADIS

CONFRONTING THE

RAGE OF ISIS

THE THEOLOGY DRIVING THE IDEOLOGY

CRAIG A. EVANS
AND
JEREMIAH J. JOHNSTON

DESTINY IMAGE® PUBLISHERS, INC.

P.O. Box 310, Shippensburg, PA 17257-0310

"Promoting Inspired Lives."

This book and all other Destiny Image and Destiny Image Fiction books are available at Christian bookstores and distributors worldwide.

Cover design by Prodigy Pixel

For more information on foreign distributors, call 717-532-3040.

Reach us on the Internet: www.destinyimage.com.

ISBN 13 TP: 978-0-7684-0899-7

ISBN 13 eBook: 978-0-7684-0900-0

For Worldwide Distribution, Printed in the U.S.A.

3 4 5 6 7 8 / 19 18 17 16

DEDICATION

To the Christians of the Middle East who have suffered at the hands of the ISIS fanatics.

> *Blessed is the man who remains steadfast under trial, for when he has stood the test he will receive the crown of life, which God has promised to those who love him* (James 1:12, ESV).

CONTENTS

INTRODUCTION

WOULD MUHAMMAD JOIN ISIS?

An Introduction to Jesus and the Jihadis

Hardly a day goes by without hearing something in the media about ISIS. Almost all that we hear is outrageous and heartbreaking. In recent weeks and months, we have heard about the looting and destruction of antiquities. Statues from the classical period have been smashed, some dating back to the seventh century BC; others have been stolen and sold on the antiquities black market. Not only that, but ancient books and manuscripts have been burned as well. These treasures from the past are irreplaceable. The ISIS vandals know no limits to the crimes against humanity that they are willing to commit.

Churches, synagogues, and monasteries have been looted and/or blown to pieces. Even some mosques have been vandalized because they contain artwork or other features that radical Muslims, including members of ISIS, do not approve of. The Associated Press has reported that eastern Christians living in Iraq have fled in the face of advancing ISIS combatants, some of them with precious books that are hundreds of years old. One codex in particular that caught our attention is a Syriac version of the letters of Paul the apostle that ISIS tried to take, which may be more than one thousand years old. If ISIS thugs got their hands on it they would have destroyed it.[1]

ISIS vandals posted a video in February 2015 depicting their enthusiastic destruction of many antiquities in a museum in Mosul, Iraq. Many of these antiquities relate to the Old Testament period, the period of Abraham and the kingdom of Israel. Winged bulls from Nineveh and Nimrud, two very important cities of the Ancient Near East, have been smashed to pieces. Reuters news service reported:

> Lamia al-Gailani, an Iraqi archaeologist and associate fellow at the London-based Institute of Archaeology, said the militants had wreaked untold damage. "It's not only Iraq's heritage: it's the whole world's," she said. "They are priceless, unique. It's unbelievable. I don't want to be Iraqi any more," she said, comparing the episode to the dynamiting of the Bamiyan Buddhas by the Afghan Taliban in 2001.[2]

Professor al-Gailani is quite correct in her assessment of the damage: "It's not only Iraq's heritage: it's the whole world's." These antiquities are irreplaceable; once destroyed, they are gone forever. And all of this is being done in the name of Allah. The perversity of it is beyond comprehension. Professor al-Gailani no longer wants to be identified as an Iraqi. Who can blame her? And one may well wonder, how many Muslims still want to be Muslim?

Inspired by ISIS atrocities, other radical Islamic groups have become more aggressive and daring than ever before. Boko Haram in Africa continues to take large numbers of school children hostage. They attack Christians wherever they can find them. They burn down churches and schools, massacring whole villages. Some of these Islamic terrorist groups raise money by taking westerners hostage for ransom. But not all hostages are released—payment or no payment—some are beheaded. They do this all in the name of Allah. And who can forget the horror of watching the video of Jordanian pilot Lt. Muah al-Kaseasbeh, who, locked in a cage, was burned to death?[3] What kind of people would do such a thing? And *why* would they do such a thing?

Why does ISIS show such violence and depravity? Why do people who say they believe in God commit such vile acts against fellow human beings, even against fellow Muslims? General William G. Boykin recently described the Islamic State as "evil in its purest form." Civilized people find the actions of ISIS and other Islamic terrorist groups horrifying and incomprehensible. But there are explanations, at least for some of it. The authors of the present volume do not pretend to know how to explain the dark hearts and twisted minds of humans who, with enthusiasm, commit such depraved crimes. But we can share with our readers the history and theology that is behind much of it.

The story goes back about 4,000 years, all the way back to one man and one place. It goes back to a decision, a choice of one son over another. This man, this place, and this choice set in motion a series of events that shaped the course of history and almost certainly will shape our future:

> *Now the Lord said to Abram, "Go from your country and your kindred and your father's house to the land that I will show you. And I will make of you a great nation, and I will bless you, and make your name great, so that you will be a blessing. I will bless those who bless you, and him who curses you I will curse; and by you all the families of the earth shall bless themselves*" (Genesis 12:1-3).

What we are seeing today in the Middle East is the direct result of a very old story, and, until it is understood, the leaders of the civilized world simply will not know how to deal with it. Therefore, this book is everything Christians (and non-Christians, for that matter) need to know about ISIS and Islam, and don't. As we will see, rather than being an un-Islamic distortion of the Qur'an and Hadith, the Islamic State adheres to and embodies the teachings of Muhammad and Islam at its core. An honest and close reading of the Islamic holy texts and traditions reveal that Muhammad would not only join the Islamic State, but he would lead it.

CHAPTER 1

AMERICANS LOVE CHICK-FIL-A; ISIS LOVES DEATH

The Islamic State Personifies Evil on a Scale Never Seen Before

"That will be twenty-four thirty-eight," said the gregarious attendant through the intercom drive-through at our local Chick-fil-A. "My pleasure to serve you at the window." As most Americans know, visiting a Chick-fil-A on a Saturday is similar to fighting crowds at Magic Kingdom in high season. This particular Saturday was no different. The drive-through lanes, which resembled midweek rush-hour traffic, required a parking attendant. Smiling faces all around. Children with shin guards, youth with baseball jerseys, and grandparents with their grandchildren. There was only one problem: they forgot the sprinkles on our kids' ice cream cones. After a conversation more akin to a hostage negotiation, my wife and I were able to convince our children going back through the line was not an option. First-world problems.

Normally I attacked the waffle fries with fervency, only this day I hesitated—$24.38 kept reverberating in my mind. I contemplated that a world away, in the city of Mosul, Iraq, an Islamic-centric, evil regime, known as the Islamic State of Iraq and Syria, was conducting their typical sex slave market day. For 25,000 Iraqi Dinars ($21.00, or a few dollars less than our lunch) a preteen Yazidi girl would be sold into sex slavery, all in the name of Allah, and sanctioned by their holy book, the Qur'an. Thousands of Yazidi women are missing at the hands of ISIS, most are enslaved, and some, seeing no way out, commit suicide.

I am reminded some things cannot be unseen. A shocking video shows ISIS mercenaries willing to pay more for sex-slave girls with blue eyes. Our daughter has blue eyes. The Qur'an is quoted, "Except those whom your right hands possess.... There is no blame on you" (4.24). I want to check my own copy of the Qur'an. Perhaps this lunatic has misquoted Islam's Holy Book. My personal copy of the Qur'an by Abdullah Yusuf Ali conveniently provides text, translation, and commentary. Ali makes clear that in Sura 4.24, women "whom your right hands possess," are "captives in a jihad, or war under the orders of the righteous Imam against those who persecute faith. In such cases formal hostility dissolves civilities." Welcome to the twenty-first century—the Islamic State.

Up to Speed on ISIS: Islam Gone Wild

The rise of the Islamic State (aka ISIS or ISIL) in the last two years and the atrocities this organization has committed have stunned the world. Child executioners, preteen wives, destruction of antiquities, crimes against humanity, genocide, killing science and progress, terror tweeting, torture, crucifixions, amputations, and slavery all in the name of Allah characterize this movement. This is carried out with the enthusiastic blessing of the caliphate—the first self-styled, self-proclaimed caliphate in nearly a hundred years.

Most people in the West have no idea what to make of it. Western leaders have been taken completely by surprise. That this group is willing to kill, and to kill brutally, to commit heinous acts against men, women, and children, is well known. What is not so well known is why they do it. Why such violence? Why do these people do such horrible things? And why do they do these things in the name of God? Are their actions true to the teachings of Islam? Their leaders and members say they are, but why do they hate Jews and Christians so much? Perhaps even more disconcerting is why there are so many young people from around the world joining ISIS. What is the attraction to this group? We must answer these questions before a solution can be found.

ISIS is the richest terrorist group in the world. At last count, ISIS has some sixty oil fields under its control and is collecting revenues of $3 million per day. But ISIS is not simply a threat in the Middle East. The FBI believes that ISIS has operatives in all fifty states in the USA. It is a growing threat abroad and at home.

"Know you are fighting men who look into the barrel of your gun and see heaven.... We are promised victory and we will surely get it," were the words cryptically incised by Dzhokhar A. Tsarnaev on the wall of a boat in Watertown, Massachusetts, where he was hiding in the days following the Boston Marathon bombing. In Dzhokhar's frenzy to evade the police, he ran over his jihadist brother with a hijacked black Mercedes. Tamerlan was wounded in a firefight with greater Boston's transit police. "I'm jealous of my brother who... received the reward of Jannutul Firdaus before me. I do not mourn because his soul is very much alive," scrawled Dzhokhar. Clearly, Dzhokhar's goal is to enter the "highest paradise" (Jannutul Firdaus) and there join the holy prophet Muhammad in eternal bliss. As the Qur'an foretells in 56.17-24:

> Round about them will serve youths of perpetual freshness, with goblets, shining beakers, and cubs filled out of clear-flowing fountains: No after-ache will they receive therefrom, nor will they suffer intoxication: And with fruits, any that they may select; and the flesh of fowls, any that they may desire. And there will be companions with beautiful, big, and lustrous eyes, like unto pearls well-guarded. A reward for the deeds of their past life.

Then again a little later on it reads:

> We have created their companions of special creation. And made them virgin-pure and undefiled, Beloved by nature, equal in age, for the companions of the right hand. (56.35-38)

Dzhokhar's chilling comment of seeing paradise in the barrel of your gun is representative of the scope and perspective of the Islamic State and their rigid adherence to the Holy Qur'an and Sharia law. We cannot effectively oppose the Islamic State without an adequate consideration of their theology, which drives their ideology. Much of the discussion, publication, and media attention have suffered from a lack of understanding of Islamic theology, which is a theology of conflict, world conquest, and domination.

In fact, there is no country on earth where large numbers of Muslims live in peace with non-Muslims. Essential to Islam is the question of how to crush and suppress unbelievers. An honest reading of the Qur'an reveals that 64 percent of its content is driven by the question of what to do with the Kafir (يثنو in Arabic—non-Muslim, infidel, unbeliever). One Islamic scholar opposes the standard use of the word "unbeliever" in place of the Islamic word Kafir because "unbeliever" is an indifferent term; rather, the Qur'an defines the Kafir as not simply one who does not accept Islam, but more descriptively as one who is "evil, disgusting, (and) the lowest form of life."[1] The political reality of Islam, according to the Qur'an, Hadith and Sira, is that the Kafir has no human or civil rights. Therefore, any non-Muslim can be killed, or worse, sold into slavery, sexually abused, raped, mistreated, dismembered, and mutilated—all sactioned by the Qur'an.

Subjugating the Kafir is not a sidebar issue in Islam. Rather, it could be demonstrably argued that terrorizing and eradicating the Kafir is a central tenant in Islam. Kafir, in all of its grammatical forms, occurs over four hundred times in the Qur'an. Furthermore, over 80 percent of the Sira, Muhammad's biography, records his struggle with the Kafir. Seventy-five percent of the Sira describes all manner of jihad and political domination, while nearly 40 percent of the Hadith is the struggle of dealing with the Kafir. The Center for the Study of Political Islam has quantitatively noted that 132,315 words are devoted to jihad in the "Islamic trilogy" of the Hadith, Sira, and Qur'an.[2] By comparison, there are slightly over 138,000 words in the Christian New Testament, which is a striking meta-narrative that nearly as many words are devoted to jihad in the holy writings of Islam.

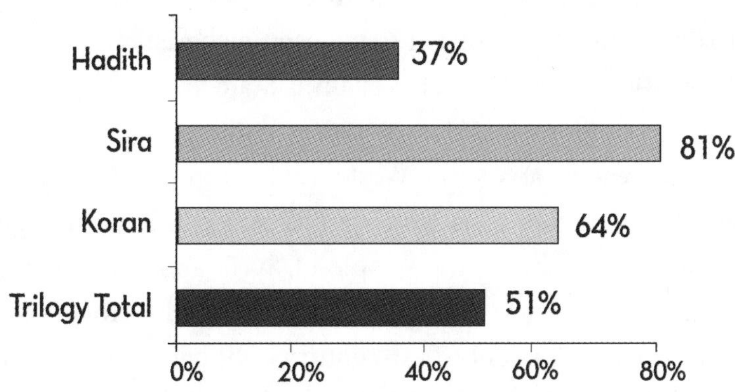

Source for graphic: http://cspipublishing.com/statistical/TrilogyStats/AmtTxtDevotedKafir.html.

The West is confused. And nowhere is this more seen than in the United States where the current president infamously remarked to *The New Yorker* that ISIS was a "jayvee" team in comparison to al-Qaeda. He even referred to ISIS as "un-Islamic," ignoring ISIS' strict adherence to their interpretation of the Holy Qur'an. Is this assessment correct? Is ISIS really un-Islamic? In reality, the Islamic State is characteristically and prototypically Islamic.

Today's Christianity suffers due to a woefully inadequate understanding of the world's second most populous religion, which is estimated at 1.6 billion Muslims globally. Christians are unaware that Jesus—only eclipsed by the prophet Muhammad—plays a central role in Islamic eschatology. According to the prophet Muhammad and Islamic tradition, Isa (Jesus) is a hero who will return (either to Damascus or Jerusalem) and defeat the Dajjal (anti-Christ figure), saving the faithful remnant of the caliphate and ushering in the day of judgment, after which Jesus will Hajj, marry, have children, and then die. Jesus is the agent who will with finality institute everlasting Sharia law (see Chapter 10 "The ISIS Endgame").

The Islamic State and Their Multi-Billion Dollar War Chest

According to the 9/11 Commission Report, the deadliest attack ever to occur on US soil cost al-Qaeda somewhere between $400,000 and $500,000 to execute. The Islamic State makes six times that amount—$3 million—per day. Notwithstanding the fact that numerous political leaders across the West have denounced the Islamic State as illegitimate, neither a state or Islamic, ISIS continues to legitimize itself while demoralizing the people of Syria and Iraq. The Islamic State is the wealthiest terrorist regime in the world. How much does it cost to operate a twenty-first-century caliphate? In January 2015, the Islamic State approved a $2 billion budget while projecting a $250 million surplus.[3] It has established its own central bank in Mosul, named the Islamic Bank, and announced plans to mint its own currency consisting of gold, silver, and copper.

Thousands of "State of the Islamic Caliphate" passports have been distributed to "citizens" across the expanse of their 35,000-square-mile controlled region. ISIS passports promise doom to anyone inflicting harm on a citizen of the caliphate: "If the holder of the passport is harmed we will deploy armies for his service." Unlike other terrorist organizations, the Islamic State has achieved multi-billion-dollar financial independence through a diversified portfolio of economic terror and multiple revenue streams. The strength of ISIS is its ability to self-finance complex and simultaneous terror initiatives via diverse revenue streams. According to a report released by the Congressional Research Service (CRS) in April 2015, ISIS is financially self-sustaining and self-perpetuating in six key areas: oil/natural gas, sale of looted antiquities on the black market, taxes/extortion/asset seizure in the name of Allah, kidnapping for ransom, external donations in an ever-increasing caliphate capital campaign, and through agriculture.

The Islamic State occupies a region larger than the countries of Jordan and Great Britain, which has allowed the regime to secure billions of dollars of revenue in oil derivatives. The International Energy Agency claimed it possessed 3 million barrels of oil with the capacity to ship 30,000 barrels per day.[4] Patrolling the porous Syria-Turkey-Iraq-Kurdish border is a near impossibility, as truckloads of crude oil are sold on the black market. ISIS has no problem selling oil to their archenemies like the Syrian Assad regime, Turkey, and the Kurds in exchange for cash or gifts in kind. The CRS points out that airstrikes by the United States and coalition forces have slowed the growth of Islamic State oil production and dissemination; however, ISIS has diversified.

Reports broadcasting the shocking images of ISIS vandalism and looting at museums across Iraq and Syria are concerning. Few are aware the second largest revenue generator for the Islamic State is the sale of looted antiquities from museums, private collections, and hundreds of archeological sites across Iraq and Syria, yielding over $100 million per year. One report revealed that over a hundred Byzantine and Roman artifacts have been smuggled by the Islamic State for sale in the United Kingdom alone.

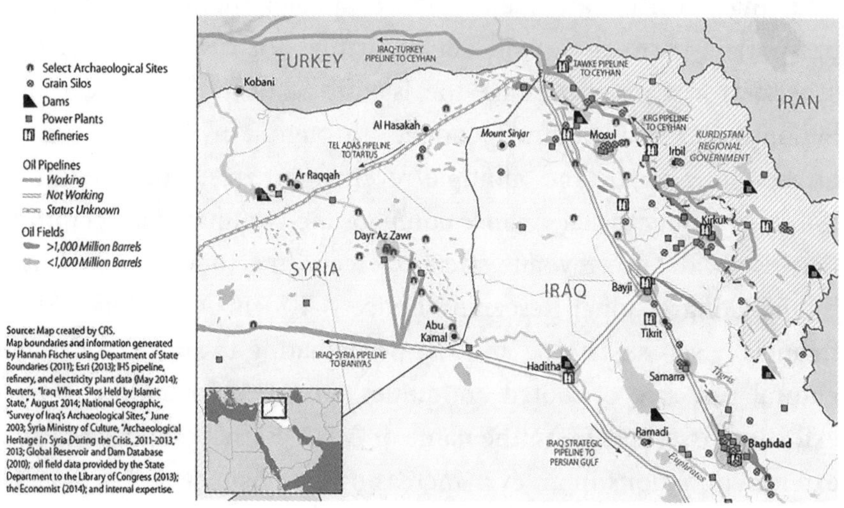

Source: Map created by CRS. Map boundaries and information generated by Hannah Fischer using Department of State Boundaries (2011); Esri (2013); IHS pipeline, refinery, and electricity plant data (May 2014); Reuters, "Iraq Wheat Silos Held by Islamic State," August 2014; National Geographic, "Survey of Iraq's Archaeological Sites," June 2003; Syria Ministry of Culture, "Archaeological Heritage in Syria During the Crisis, 2011-2013," 2013; Global Reservoir and Dam Database (2010); oil field data provided by the State Department to the Library of Congress (2013); the Economist (2014); and internal expertise.

ISIS robs banks on an epic scale that makes Public Enemy Number 1, John Dillinger, look like an altar boy (Dillinger allegedly robbed more than twenty banks). Sixty-two Iraqi banks were seized across sixteen cities, including Mosul, Tikrit, and Fallujah, rendering the Islamic State a cool $500 million in cash. Corruption, extreme taxation, and asset seizure are hallmarks of the Islamic State's internal financing. ISIS has instituted the Islamic tithe, known as *zakat* (Sura 2.43, 110, 177, 277; 9.5). All businesses, from mobile phone companies to farmers or commercial shops, operating in ISIS territories are required to pay a percentage of their earnings to the caliphate, generating an estimated $168–228 million per month. Students from elementary through university are taxed monthly to continue educational pursuits. Following the guidelines prescribed by Muhammad in Qur'an 9.29, Christians are required to pay the humiliating jizya tax as a reminder of their inferior status. Not all religious groups are so lucky, however. The Yazidis, for example, are unlucky—unlike the Jewish–Christian groups, they are regarded a polytheists and therefore executed or enslaved with no option of paying jizya.

Kidnapping and ransom continue to be a significant revenue driver for the Islamic State as well. The United Nations reported ISIS extorted nearly $50 million in ransom fees in 2014 alone. For example, the CRS reported that France might have paid $18 million to recover four of its captured journalists in April of 2014. Last year, nearly 200,000 refugees migrated from Africa and the Middle East, many of them aided by ISIS militants, generating over $300 million for the Islamic State.

The Islamic State has amassed significant revenue through donations as well, generating $40 million in 2013–2014 alone. Millions of dollars in external support have flowed into it from sympathizers in Saudi Arabia, Qatar, and Kuwait. The CRS stated that the Islamic State is also profiting off of agriculture, trading wheat and barley, generating upwards of $200 million per year for their cause.

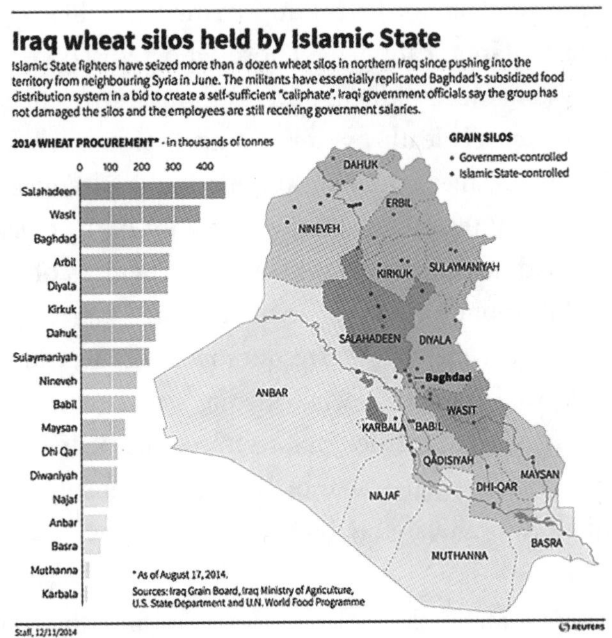

Image found at: http://www.businessinsider.com/tafrikinomics-how-isis-funds-its-caliphate-2015-3

With strict adherence to the Qur'an, the Islamic State continues to finance their genocidal activities with the swagger of mobsters in an organized crime syndicate. It steals, cheats, pilfers, swindles, extorts, skims, loots, victimizes, defrauds, robs, traffics, and racketeers all in the name of Allah. And the Qur'an endorses economic oppression:

> So enjoy what you took as booty; the spoils are lawful and good. (Qur'an 8.69)
>
> And He caused you to inherit their land and their houses and their wealth, and land ye have not trodden. Allah is ever Able to do all things. (Qur'an 33.27)
>
> But (now) enjoy what ye took in war, lawful and good. (Qur'an 8.69)

Islam Means Surrender, Not Peace

There is little doubt that calls for jihad from the Ottoman dynasty influenced the genocide of 1.5 million Armenian Christians in 1915, during the last Islamic caliphate. Those who refused conversion to Islam were systematically killed. Several thousand women and children escaped a cruel death by converting to Islam. In less than a decade (1914–1922), the Armenian population was reduced from 2.1 million to just 387,000. Islam should have a lot on its conscience. In 1,400 years, jihad has conservatively claimed the lives of 260 million innocents. Philosopher George Santayana once warned that those who cannot learn from history are doomed to repeat it. As a more sophisticated, well-funded, social media savvy, extremely brutal caliphate emerges, what further lessons must we learn? In view of the evidence and horrors perpetrated by ISIS, it is an insult that so many of the media and political elite have referred to the Islamic State as "un-Islamic."

Is the Islamic State Islamic or not? Yes, in fact, the Islamic State is quintessentially Qur'an-centric. Consider the following passages from the Qur'an and compare these passages with the brutality of the Islamic State that we read about in newspapers or hear about today:

> So when you meet in battle those who disbelieve, then smite the necks until when you have overcome them, then make (them) prisoners. (47.4)

> The punishment of those who wage war against Allah and His Messenger, and strive with might and main for mischief through the land is: execution, or crucifixion, or the cutting off of hands and feet from opposite sides, or exile from the land: that is their disgrace in this world, and a heavy punishment is theirs in the Hereafter. (5.33)

There are four passages in the Qur'an that encourage sexual slavery of kidnapped women, two or which are quoted below:

> Fight in the cause of Allah those who fight you, but do not transgress limits; for Allah loveth not transgressors. And slay them wherever ye catch them, and turn them out from where they have Turned you out; for tumult and oppression are worse than slaughter; but fight them not at the Sacred Mosque, unless they (first) fight you there; but if they fight you, slay them. Such is the reward of those who suppress faith. (2.190-91)

> Warfare is ordained for you, though it is hateful unto you; but it may happen that ye hate a thing which is good for you, and it may happen that ye love a thing which is bad for you. Allah knoweth, ye know not. (2.216)

In total there are over a hundred verses in the Qur'an enjoining Muslims to fight, kill, torture, rape, pillage, and conquer in the name of Allah against the Kafir. Additionally, in the Bukhari Hadith (Islam's most dependable Hadith) there are over two hundred references attributed to Muhammad related to jihad. Despite what western relativistic thinking has dogmatically said, all religions are not the same—they are not equal. The Islamic god does not love everyone. In Islam equality is the privilege of the few not the God-given right of all: "Muhammad is the messenger of Allah; and those who are with him are strong against Unbelievers, (but) compassionate amongst each other" (Qur'an 48.29).

Current opinions about ISIS often suffer from a "politically correct" notion focused on this group's ideology while ignoring its theology. We cannot properly assess ISIS ideology without taking into account ISIS theology. Major General Michael K. Nagata, of the Special Operations forces in the Middle East, stated, "We do not understand the movement, and until we do, we are not going to defeat it."[5] In this book we seek to take a fresh look at the shocking events that are happening around the world and explain the theological underpinnings motivating the "why" question. As historians and biblical scholars, our aim is to guide the reader by the hand through the halls of history, demonstrating how the violence and extremism of terrorist groups like ISIS are rooted in a deeply flawed understanding of God and the human condition. Most Christians do not know how to respond to the growing ISIS threat. How would Jesus react to the jihadis? Ignoring ISIS is not an option.

Unfortunately, this problem is not going away. Mike Morrell, a thirty-three-year veteran of the CIA and former acting director, calls our conflict with ISIS a "great war" that promises to extend for "as far as I can see." Gen. Martin Dempsey, chairman of the Joint Chiefs of Staff, says the US-led conflict with ISIS will last for "years." Voices throughout the government and defense forces are saying we should prepare for a years-long conflict fighting the Islamic State. After stating that we are at war with ISIS, Secretary of State John Kerry said, "Our commitment (opposing ISIS) will be measured most likely in years." Western powers are engaging an enemy that has theological and eternal motivations to desire death in the name of jihad.

The Islamic State is a culture in love with devastation. ISIS has created a socio-ecological system which loves death more than the West loves life. It is a theologically enhanced ideology that "sees heaven in the barrel of a gun." The Islamic State is Islamic by de facto, with a mindset completely foreign to the values of Western civilization. In the face of the foremost evil of our time, the words of Jesus of Nazareth are urgently needed, "I came that they may have life, and have it abundantly" (John 10:10). We turn now to the land where the three great Abrahamic faiths emerged, the land of Israel.

CHAPTER 2

THE EXODUS AND THE CONQUEST

The Fight for the Land Begins

It's one thing to be promised land, but it's quite another to get it and actually hold onto it. In the days of Abraham (*c.* 2,000 BC) the Promised Land (today's Israel) was something of a frontier. There were peoples scattered here and there, with tribal chieftains who governed over small territories. There were kingdoms, to be sure, but they were far away to the east and northeast, and not so far away in Egypt to the south. But in the time of Abraham's descendants, several centuries later (*c.* 1,500 BC), for the Hebrew people who lived in Egypt, in the territory known as Goshen, a lot had changed.

Escape from Egypt: The Story of the Exodus

Egypt had grown larger and was more aware of aggressive, expanding kingdoms in the Middle East, even though Egypt was pretty aggressive herself. The Promised Land was occupied by a number of warlike fiefdoms, such as the Philistines (near the Mediterranean Sea), the Jebusites (in the Judean hills, centered in what would become Jerusalem), the Canaanites, and the Amalekites, as well as a few other tribes. Treaties and alliances linked various kingdoms and, in some cases, led to war. Most of the smaller kingdoms were allied to one or the other of the bigger ones.

Beliefs about the gods played an important role in these treaties and alliances. That may sound strange to us who live in modern times, but in great antiquity the gods were called upon as witnesses and, if a treaty was broken, avengers. Of course, the bigger and more impressive your gods, the greater the leverage in making a treaty. Again, this may sound strange to us moderns, but in antiquity polytheism (the belief in many gods) was commonplace. Not only were there many gods, but those gods were regional. This means there were gods of Egypt, gods of Babylon, and gods of a variety of other smaller kingdoms and fiefdoms. When a major power reached out and annexed a smaller kingdom, the smaller kingdom was expected to adopt the gods of the greater kingdom. So it wasn't just human kingdoms and armies that opposed one another—the gods took sides too.

It should be mentioned that the gods did not exist to benefit humanity; rather, humanity served the gods. Simply put, the gods had their needs and humans were required to meet those needs. This was the purpose of temples and religion in great antiquity—to placate the gods and, if possible, to persuade them to protect the people who worshiped and served them. As expressed in an ancient Canaanite text, when a sacrifice was offered on an altar, the gods smelled and consumed the smoke, which was their "food." Offering the gods food, giving them houses to live in, and showing them honor was all part of the polytheism of the time. If the gods were well cared for, the people who worshiped them could hope for abundant crops, livestock, good health, and prosperity.

But the big gods needed big temples and shrines in which to live and in which to be worshiped. Divine kings and pharaohs, who were closely linked to these gods and in a sense were even "adopted" by the gods, needed big temples too, which usually took the form of great monumental tombs. For the Egyptians, this sometimes meant great pyramids were erected. Consequently, there were a lot of big building projects, which in turn meant there was need for a great deal of labor, and cheap labor at that. And that is where the slaves came in.

The Hebrew people had prospered and grown numerous in the land of Egypt. Although initially welcomed in Egypt, the shift in politics caused the Egyptian government to view these resident foreigners with suspicion. One fear was that the Hebrew people might ally themselves with another foreign people against Egypt. Consequently, Egypt's king (called Pharaoh) kept a tight leash on the Hebrew people, greatly restricting their freedoms and essentially enslaving them. This enslavement largely involved taking part in the building of Pharaoh's great monuments, probably including the famous pyramids, as well as other tombs and temples.

Long after their escape from servitude in Egypt, the Hebrew people recalled those hard times. In the Bible, in a book called Exodus, which tells the story of the Hebrew people's escape from Egypt, we find references to making bricks. Pharaoh is so concerned that the Hebrew people will become disloyal to him and to his gods that he makes their work even harder, forcing them to make bricks without providing them with straw:

> *You shall no longer give the people straw to make bricks, as heretofore; let them go and gather straw for themselves. But the number of bricks which they made heretofore you shall lay upon them, you shall by no means lessen it; for they are idle; therefore they cry, "Let us go and offer sacrifice to our God"* (Exodus 5:7-8).

The Hebrew people had to gather their own straw (which before had been provided for them) and yet still meet the daily quota of making bricks. Failure to meet the quota meant punishment, such as beatings. The situation was impossible.

It was in this setting that Moses arose. Through a fluke, the young Moses was raised in the household of Pharaoh and was accorded every privilege. But the oppression of his people proved too much for him. One day he struck down an Egyptian who was beating a Hebrew slave and fled into the wilderness when he learned that he had been found out. It was in the wilderness that Moses met God in the famous encounter with the burning bush.

It was at this bush that Moses met the God without a name. All of the other gods of the peoples of great antiquity had names. The Babylonians worshiped Marduk and others, while the Egyptians worshiped Anubis, Horus, Ra, and Isis, among others. All of these gods had names. But the God Moses met did not have a name…well, not exactly.

When Moses approached the burning bush, God identified himself: "I am the God of your father, the God of Abraham, the God of Isaac, and the God of Jacob" (Exodus 3:6). Then here God commissions Moses to confront Pharaoh with the demand that the Hebrew people be allowed to depart from Egypt and have the freedom to worship God rather than the gods of the Egyptians. Moses then wants to know God's name: "If I come to the people of Israel and say to them, 'The God of your fathers has sent me to you,' and they ask me, 'What is his name?' what shall I say to them?" (Exodus 3:13). It is a reasonable question. After all, gods—like humans—have names. But God replied in a very unexpected way: "I AM WHO I AM…. Say this to the people of Israel, 'I AM has sent me to you'" (Exodus 3:14).

This remarkable reply has fascinated historians and scholars of religion for millennia. God simply has no name, at least not in the conventional sense. He is not "Ra" or "Marduk" or "Anubis." He is absolute and wholly unique. He is God, and there is no other like him. The gods of the pagans are nothing more than distortions of the true God, a mere shattering and splintering of his deity and power, as it were. The uniqueness of God, the fact that there is no other god, means that God has no need for a "name" that distinguishes him from other the gods. God is simply the "One Who Is." He is the one who exists.

Because the Hebrew word for "he is" or "he exists" is *yahweh* (the word that appears in Exodus 3), the God of the Bible is regularly identified as Yahweh, as though it is a proper name. In the Greek, this name is regularly translated as *kyrios*, which means "Lord." In fact, because "Yahweh" is so sacred that devout Jews are reluctant to speak it, the Hebrew word *adonai*, which also means "Lord," is often used in its place. But the important thing to remember is that the God of the Bible, the God of the patriarchs Abraham, Isaac, and Jacob, has no name like the other gods of great antiquity. He is simply the "One Who Is," the ground of all being, the Creator and Sustainer of all life.

Inspired and empowered by the God of the Hebrews, Moses confronts Pharaoh and the excitement begins. The plagues, the wild escape from Egypt on Passover night, and the destruction of Pharaoh's army in the sea make for great reading. It's a shame that the producers of the movie *Exodus: Gods and Kings* tried to improve on the story. I have to agree with the critics—the book is much better.

The Quest for Homeland Security: Conquest of the Promised Land

The quest of finding one's own land was in fact a quest for homeland security: to find a land where a people could live in security and call home. The story of the Promised Land (Israel) is just that story. As we explained in the Introduction, the quest for a land the Hebrew people could call their own began with the founding patriarch Abraham and his long-suffering wife, Sarah. God had promised them land, posterity, and blessing. But when would they and their multitudinous descendants receive it?

Centuries had passed. The Hebrews had migrated to Egypt, whose fertile Nile valley was nourished by its famous river, which every year overflowed its banks and thus rejuvenated the black soil for another season of crops. But this long sojourn had come to a sudden and dramatic end. Under the leadership of Moses, the Hebrews had fled Egypt and now found themselves in the Sinai wilderness, in what was essentially no-man's-land. What now?

It's hardly surprising that the people grumbled in this place. In fact, the people's grumbling and murmuring against Moses becomes thematic in the wilderness narratives. The upside to the new situation was not readily apparent. The downside certainly was. After all, despite the hardships that their Egyptian taskmasters had placed on them, the Hebrew people at least had homes and fertile soil in which they could grow their cucumbers, melons, and leeks. The hot, dry desert was anything but accommodating.

The sour, ungrateful, and grumbling attitude of the Hebrew people resulted in wandering in the wilderness a lot longer than originally planned. The sojourn in this desert lasted for an entire generation. What makes the grumblers look especially bad is their ingratitude and fecklessness. God provided the people manna (literally meaning, "What is it?"), water, and quail for meat. The Israelites never starved and they did not die of thirst. When attacked they were able to defend themselves.

Perhaps the most disgraceful event of the wilderness period was what happened at Mount Sinai, where God made a covenant with his people. While Moses was on the mountain for some days, the people foolishly decided to make a golden idol, a calf on which the god would sit (Exodus 32:1-6). In doing this, they were just like the Egyptians and other pagan nations of antiquity. The only kind of god they could imagine was a god of their own making, a god they could see with their own eyes. What made this sorry event especially horrible was that it was Aaron himself, the brother of Moses, who supervised the making of the idol.

When Moses came down from the mountain and saw what the people had done, he was so incensed that he broke the stone tablets, signifying that Israel had broken their covenant with God. God was so angry with Israel that he was ready to destroy the people and start over with Moses. God relented, however, and gave foolish Israel another chance. Moses was so overcome with this grace that he begs to see God's face. He is told, however: "You cannot see my face; for man shall not see me and live" (Exodus 33:20). Nevertheless, God does permit Moses to catch a fleeting glimpse of his "back."

Two new tablets of stone are prepared. Then God passes by, proclaiming: "The LORD, the LORD, a God merciful and gracious, slow to anger, and abounding in steadfast love and faithfulness, keeping steadfast love for thousands, forgiving iniquity and transgression and sin..." (Exodus 34:6-7). Israel has been forgiven. The covenant has been restored, and all because God is gracious and forgiving. Without question, this is one of the greatest passages in all of the Old Testament, for it sounds a theme that runs throughout the Bible: God is gracious, loving, and restorative.

God is no ogre who takes delight in punishing the wicked or making the lives of people miserable. He is not like the gods of the pagans, who are indifferent toward humans. Yahweh, the God who is, cares for his creation and is especially interested in humanity, for of all creatures it is only the human who is made "in the image of God" and so has infinite worth (Genesis 1:27). Nevertheless, willful disobedience and disrespect often have negative consequences. For the first generation of Hebrews who escaped Egypt, there was no escaping the wilderness and there was no entry into the land that God long ago had promised to give them.

After forty years and the passing of the original generation in the wilderness, a new generation of Hebrews was ready to be led across the Jordan River into the Promised Land, the land of Canaan as it was then known. Joshua, the successor of Moses and one of only two survivors of the first generation, brought the people into the land on the west side of the Jordan. Before him the walls of Jericho fell down and several chieftains were defeated. Under the dynamic leadership of Joshua, most of the land promised to Abraham was occupied and settled. At least two of the promises made to Abraham were now fulfilled—they possessed land and had a multitude of descendants.

The conquest of the Promised Land was not easy, however. Under the leadership of Joshua, the Hebrew people—called *Israel* after the great patriarch Jacob whose name had been changed to Israel—formed an army that almost always was victorious in the field of battle. Israel fought its way into the West Bank, an area of real estate that was as controversial then as it is today. Some tribes agreed to become part of the advancing people, while other tribes fought and were defeated. Much of the land was conquered.

Near the end of his life, Joshua summoned all of Israel's leaders together (Joshua 24). He reminded them of how God had brought his people out of Egypt, how he had guided them through the wilderness, and how he had gone before them as they entered and took possession of the land of Canaan, a land promised long ago to Israel's founding father Abraham. He ends his farewell speech by admonishing the people to put away their idols and their tendency to worship the gods of the pagans. He urges them to remain loyal to Yahweh, the God who is, concluding his speech with an ultimatum: "Choose this day whom you will serve, whether the gods your fathers served in the region beyond the River, or the gods of the Amorites in whose land you dwell; but as for me and my house, we will serve the LORD" (Joshua 24:15). The people responded by saying, "Far be it from us that we should forsake the LORD, to serve other gods" (Joshua 24:16).

They meant what they said, but their children and grandchildren didn't necessarily share the same convictions and commitments. In the years that followed, which are the periods of the judges and the kings, the people of Israel experienced many ups and downs. At the center of their struggle was the land and the peoples who still lived within it, peoples who worshiped idols and encouraged Israel to do likewise. Israel had a long way to go.

Expectation for a Messiah

Throughout Israel's history, Israel would rise and fall again, be taken into captivity and eventually restored to her land. Though the history is tumultuous at best, there were many prophecies of a Messiah who would come and restore all things. But Messianic expectation was not limited to the interpretation of prophecies; some of this expectation took very active and aggressive forms. A number of men at various times rose up and proclaimed themselves to be prophets, kings, or messiahs of one sort or another. And a few of these men actually enjoyed a measure of success, at least for a while. All promised change and all were eventually defeated and killed. In many cases the Jewish people suffered greatly because of these bids for power.

The would-be kings and messiahs continued to make their appearance, even during and after Herod's autocratic rule. But not all was bad. Israel prospered and the magnificent sanctuary and temple complex were constructed. What stability there was ended when Herod died in 4 BC (or possibly 1 BC [the chronology is uncertain]). His surviving three sons lacked their father's strength and skills. His oldest son, Archelaus, received the southern half of the kingdom, made up of Samaria and Judea. Archelaus was appointed ethnarc ("ruler of the people"), and was as incompetent as he was ruthless, so not surprisingly a Roman governor replaced him in AD 6. His two younger brothers, Philip and Antipas, fared better. Both were given the titles tetrarch ("ruler of one fourth"). Philip ruled in the northeast, including the territory east of Galilee called Gaulanitis (today's Golan Heights). Antipas ruled Galilee, the land in which Jesus grew up and was active as a public figure. It was into this world that Jesus was born.

The world of Jesus was complicated, difficult, and dangerous. Yet it was the world he entered "in the fullness of time" to accomplish God's saving work. Who was this Jesus? What did he teach and what did he do? It is important we understand that importance of Jesus, for he is a key figure in the teachings of Islam.

CHAPTER 3

A PERSON OF INTEREST

The Life and Death of Jesus the Messiah

Jesus grew up in Nazareth, a small village in Galilee about sixteen miles west of the southwest shore of the Sea of Galilee. Four miles northwest of Nazareth is Sepphoris, a city expanded and much improved in the early first century during the administration of Herod Antipas, the tetrarch of Galilee. It is possible, though by no means certain, that Jesus and his brothers, and perhaps Joseph, Mary's husband who was a builder, worked in Sepphoris too.

Archaeological excavations in the last thirty years or so have revealed the grandeur of Sepphoris. In Jesus's time it had been built into a Greco-Roman style city with paved, colonnaded streets. However, the population of the city was Jewish, and this Jewish population observed the major tenets of the Jewish faith. We know this because no non-kosher animal bones have been found in the city (dating to the time of Jesus), nor have pagan images or buildings for uses contrary to Jewish morals been found. But we have found stone water vessels, which were important to the Jewish people for purification (John 2:6), and *miqvoth*, or ritual immersion pools, which were also very important for personal hygiene and purification according to Jewish laws and customs (Leviticus 15–16).

We have no reason to believe that the Jewish people who lived in villages in Galilee were any less observant of the laws of Moses. Nazareth itself probably had no more than a few hundred inhabitants. The village being situated on a ridge, there is evidence of terrace farming, viticulture (growing grapes for the production of wine), and building. Joseph was called a "builder" (sometimes translated "carpenter" [Matthew 13:55]); so was Jesus (Mark 6:3). The evidence so far suggests that Nazareth was not a sleepy village whose men had to seek employment in nearby Sepphoris or elsewhere. Rather, Nazareth probably enjoyed an active economy, which would have included trade.

Of great interest to Christians has been the discovery of three houses that date to the first century BC and first century AD. Because Nazareth is a living modern city, with a population of about 65,000, archaeological excavations are understandably limited. However, excavations beneath the ruins of two Byzantine-era (fourth-century) churches have uncovered the foundations, floors, steps, and lower portions of walls of two houses, one thought to have belonged to the family of Mary, the mother of Jesus, and the other thought to have been the home of Mary and Joseph and their children, including Jesus and his brother James. The modern Basilica of the Annunciation now stands over the house of Mary, while the modern Sisters of Nazareth convent stands over the house thought to have belonged to Mary and Joseph, a house that was abandoned sometime in the first century. This is consistent with early church history that says Mary and James (and perhaps other siblings) relocated to Jerusalem. A third house was recently uncovered across the street from the Basilica of the Annunciation. Whether or not it was related to Mary's house is not clear.

The archaeological evidence, such as it is, supports the view that although the village of Nazareth was small, it enjoyed a standard of living that was comparable to that enjoyed by most people in villages and rural settings.[1] The history of Nazareth itself is of interest. There is no mention of the village until the first century AD. This is probably because the village was founded in the first or second century BC as part of the effort to "re-Judaize" Galilee and other territories that had at one time been part of the kingdom of Israel (1 Maccabees 15:33-34). Many of the Jews who entered Galilee in the first century were from Judea and many of them were from the tribes of Judah, Benjamin, and Levi.

As Europeans in later times settled in the Americas, they named many of their cities after those they left behind in the old world, so the Judeans who settled in Galilee named some of their villages after the villages they left behind in the south. Accordingly, we have a Bethlehem in Galilee, a Cana of Galilee, and a few other examples as well. Nazareth was one of these new Galilean villages, and the name "Nazareth" was new too, so far as we know. The name was probably a deliberate allusion to the *nezer*, or "branch" of Jesse the father of David, that is mentioned in the messianic prophecy of Isaiah: "There shall come forth a shoot from the stump of Jesse, and a branch (*nezer*) shall grow out of his roots. And the Spirit of the LORD shall rest upon him..." (Isaiah 11:1-2). Jesse and his family, including his famous son David, were from Bethlehem of Judea. When people in Bethlehem in the first or second century BC relocated to Galilee, they named their new village after their beloved and famous ancestral home.

This in turn provides a context for understanding Joseph's southward journey from Nazareth in Galilee to Bethlehem in Judea in response to the census. In all probability he had family and property and/or financial interests in Bethlehem, the city from which his father or grandfather had come. Even Mary herself likely had family in or near Bethlehem too. The "Christmas" journey to Bethlehem, at which time Jesus was born (Matthew 2; Luke 2), was probably one trip among many (Luke 2:41 where it mentions this trip was "every year"). We hear of Jesus at the age of twelve in Jerusalem (Luke 2:42-51). It is probable that while growing up, as well as in his later public ministry, Jesus traveled between Galilee and Judea on several occasions (as implied in John's Gospel, where three different Passover visits to Jerusalem are mentioned).

Radical skeptics, including the so-called "mythicists" (those who assert that Jesus of Nazareth was not a real person), will sometimes claim that there was no village in Galilee named Nazareth. They claim that Nazareth is nothing more than a Christian invention to provide the mythical Jesus a hometown. They feel justified in making this extraordinary claim because the first-century Jewish historian Josephus, who mentions the names of many cities and villages in Israel, never mentions Nazareth by name. These skeptics point out, moreover, that no non-Christian source refers to Nazareth.

This radical skepticism flies in the face of reason and probability. After all, it would be hard enough to convince people in the first century that a nonexistent first-century Jesus had really existed and had actually been a prominent public figure who died in a violent and public way in Jerusalem. But how difficult would it be to convince first-century Jews in Galilee that this nonexistent Jesus came from a nonexistent village, not too far from the Sea of Galilee? The whole notion is purely absurd. The lack of literary references to Nazareth is because it was a small village and had not been in existence for long. It played no strategic role in the great Jewish rebellion against Rome in AD 66–70. In fact, the only person of significance ever to come from Nazareth was Jesus himself.

It is inconceivable that members and supporters of the Jesus movement—never mind critics of the Jesus movement—would not have discovered that there really was no village of Nazareth if in fact it had been the case. This is even more apparent in the case of Jesus himself. Is it really credible to think that supporters and critics alike would not have discovered that there really had been no Jesus of Nazareth? There were plenty of critics of Jesus and his followers, but no critic until modern times ever suggested that there never had been a Jesus of history or a Nazareth of history.

Of course, there is archaeological evidence for a real Nazareth. We don't refer to the archaeological excavations that continue in and around Nazareth; we refer to an inscription in which the name "Nazareth" appears. It was discovered in 1962 in the vicinity of the ruins of a third or fourth century AD Jewish synagogue in the city of Caesarea Maritima (on the Mediterranean coast, the city where the Romans who governed Israel resided). What was discovered was a dark marble slab, on which were inscribed the priestly courses (based on 1 Chronicles 24:15-16). There were four lines, the second of which reads: "The eighteenth course is Happizzez of Nazareth." Nazareth certainly did exist. If Christians had "invented" it as part of a Jesus myth, why would the Jewish leaders of a synagogue refer to it? Even more, why would one of the priestly courses, in the aftermath of the Jewish rebellions and loss of the temple that required reorganization, relocate to a nonexistent village? The whole idea is silly.

We have taken the time to say something about archaeology because of the important role it often plays in clarifying and confirming statements in old texts and narratives, like those found in the Bible. The reason archaeologists and scholars—whether Jewish or Christian or those of no faith—take the Gospels and other narratives in the Bible seriously is because archaeology and other external sources provide corroboration. Again and again, archaeology and other sources show that the Gospels and biblical narratives are talking about real people, real places, and real events that actually happened in real time. These narratives are not fairy tales, as some radical but uninformed critics sometimes claim.

This observation will come into play later in this book, as we compare Islamic teaching and various statements in the Qur'an with what is said in the Gospels and other parts of the Bible. We will find that almost always there is no archaeological, geographical, or topographical correlation with the distinctive claims made in the Qur'an and in other Islamic traditions.

Another important indication that the Gospels are telling us about a real person, a man who grew up in Nazareth and then as an adult traveled about in Galilee, preaching, teaching, and healing, is that what they tell us squares with what we know of the history of this time and place. We hear of Antipas and Philip, sons of Herod the Great, men who became tetrarchs of the northern parts of Israel. We read of Herod the Great himself. We read of Roman governors like Pontius Pilate (and other Roman governors in the New Testament's book of Acts). We hear of Jewish high priests like Annas and his son-in-law Caiaphas.[2] We read of real places, such as Capernaum, the Sea of Galilee, Cana of Galilee, Chorazin of Galilee, and Bethsaida of Gaulanitis. We read of Samaria to the south and Judea further south. We read of the Jordan River and the ancient city of Jericho. We not only hear of the famous city of Jerusalem but also the small surrounding villages of Bethany and Bethphage. Fictional accounts that speak of nonexistent legendary people, written by authors who do not know what they are talking about or who have no commitment to telling the truth, could not write narratives such as these.

What triggered the public preaching of Jesus was the arrest of his associate John the Baptist or "baptizer" (literally "immerser"). John called on the Jewish people to repent, warning them that God was about to begin a powerful work in Israel and beyond. As a demonstration of their repentance, the people were immersed by John in the Jordan River and in other bodies of water (Matthew 3:1-12; Mark 1:2-8; Luke 3:1-20; John 1:19-28). For the Jewish people, ritual immersion signified cleansing and purification. It probably meant this for John also, but immersing people in the Jordan River recalled the original crossing of the Jordan under the leadership of Joshua long ago. Crossing the Jordan signified entry into the Promised Land. Being baptized in the Jordan by John symbolized the restoration of Israel and a new beginning for Israel. Jesus himself went to John and was baptized (Matthew 3:13-17; Mark 1:9-11; Luke 3:21-22), thereby affirming the importance of John's ministry.

But John called on everyone to repent, including the tetrarch Herod Antipas (Matthew 14:3-4; Mark 6:17-18; Luke 3:19). John was especially angry with the Galilean ruler because he betrayed his wife and became romantically involved with his sister-in-law Herodias, who was the wife of Philip. The actions of Antipas and Herodias were scandalous and created a political crisis, for the jilted wife of Antipas was the daughter of Aretas, the king of Nabatea, a kingdom immediately to the east of Israel. When John condemned Antipas for his adulterous actions, he was pouring gas on the fire. Not surprisingly, Antipas imprisoned John in order to silence him and get him out of public view. Goaded by Herodias, Antipas eventually had John executed (Matthew 14:5-11; Mark 6:19-28; Josephus, *Ant.* 18.116-19).

Shortly after the arrest of John the Baptist, Jesus began to proclaim the good news of the kingdom of God (Mark 1:14-15). There is no question that his message was based on the prophecy of Isaiah, in which a beleaguered Israel was encouraged to lift up her voice and shout for joy, for salvation was at hand. The reason for rejoicing was because God had made himself known and felt: "Behold your God!" (Isaiah 40:9). In the Aramaic paraphrase of Scripture, which in the time of Jesus was taking shape in the synagogue, "Behold your God" became "The kingdom of your God has been revealed."

Jesus proclaimed that God's kingdom or rule had come (Isaiah 52:7), which was the "good news" or gospel (Isaiah 61:1-2). He demonstrated the truth and reality of his proclamation through his remarkable teaching and even more remarkable works of power. When asked by messengers sent by the imprisoned John if he truly was the awaited coming one, Jesus replied: "Go and tell John what you hear and see: the blind receive their sight and the lame walk, lepers are cleansed and the deaf hear, and the dead are raised up, and the poor have good news preached to them" (Matthew 11:4-5).

All of Jesus's teaching reflected the central truth of his proclamation: the rule of God was at hand. People needed to repent and respond in faith. Many did, lives were changed, and soon large crowds followed Jesus. Jesus taught his disciples to pray: "Our Father who art in heaven, hallowed be thy name. Thy kingdom come, thy will be done, on earth as it is in heaven" (Matthew 6:9-10). Through the ministry of Jesus, God's will began to unfold on the earth. Jesus forgave sinners and taught his disciples to do likewise. He urged his followers to pray for their enemies and to share with those in need.

Jesus told parables that illustrated his understanding of God and the expectations that God has for his people. The well-known parable of the Good Samaritan (Luke 10:30-39) teaches that a person's neighbor who must be loved is the individual who is near and in need and not just those who are family and friends. The parable of the great banquet (Luke 14:15-24) teaches that the affluent might not inherit eternal life, whereas the apparent poor and unblessed might. The parable of the prodigal son (Luke 15:11-32) likewise teaches that the forgiveness of a brother who repents does not diminish the brother who is righteous. And the parable of the rich man and the poor man (Luke 16:19-30) teaches that wealth is not proof of righteousness and poverty is not proof of unrighteousness.

It was not surprising that when Jesus took his dynamic message and his life-changing teaching into the city of Jerusalem and into the precincts of the holy temple, those who preferred the status quo felt threatened. The ruling priests and their supporters, the most powerful Jewish men in Israel, challenged Jesus. Jewish sources from this approximate time reveal that the ruling priests (but not the village priests) were very unpopular with most of the people. They were accused of avarice, insensitivity toward the plight of the poor (whom, according to the law of Moses, they were supposed to protect and support), corruption, and violence.

When confronted by the ruling priests, Jesus warned that their authority and their position were in danger of being taken away from them. In his well-known parable of the wicked vineyard tenants (Mark 12:1-12), Jesus implied that the ruling priests were murderers and that they would murder God's Son (Jesus) as surely as their ancestors had murdered some of the prophets long ago. The ruling priests were furious and began plotting ways of killing Jesus (and in doing this they evidently unwittingly showed that they were indeed murderous).

Late at night, while in prayer on the Mount of Olives, guards and thugs acting under the orders of the ruling priests seized Jesus. He was taken to Caiaphas the high priest and his father-in-law Annas, a former high priest who was still very much the power "behind the throne." Jesus was accused of many things, but the accusations didn't stick. Finally, an angry and frustrated Caiaphas asked Jesus, "Are you the Christ, the Son of the Blessed?" (Mark 14:61), or, in more conventional language, "Are you the Messiah, the Son of God?" Jesus replied that indeed he was, adding, "You will see the Son of man seated at the right hand of Power, and coming with the clouds of heaven" (Mark 14:62).

Caiaphas and his colleagues rightly understood the import of Jesus's words, which alluded to two powerful Old Testament passages (Psalm 110:1 and Daniel 7:9-14). Not only did he claim to be the Messiah, the very Son of God, but he also claimed that the next time the high priest saw him, he would be seated on God's throne, next to God himself. He who is currently being judged will someday return and judge his judges. Not surprisingly, Caiaphas was indignant, crying out, "Why do we still need witnesses? You have heard his blasphemy. What is your decision?" (Mark 14:63-64). They all agreed—Jesus should be put to death.

The following morning a majority of the Jewish council accepted the recommendation of the ruling priests and sent Jesus to the Roman governor Pontius Pilate. When assured that condemning Jesus to death would not put him in a difficult spot politically, Pilate ordered his crucifixion as "King of the Jews" (Mark 15:1-15,

26). The language was that of Rome, which had some seventy years earlier appointed Herod the "king of the Jews" (Josephus, *War* 1.388, where Herod says to emperor Augustus: "I was made king of the Jews by Antony."). This was not the language of the ruling priests, who mocked the suffering Jesus, "Let the Christ, the King of Israel, come down now from the cross, that we may see and believe" (Mark 15:32), nor was it the language of the early Christian church, which confessed Jesus as Lord and Son of God (Acts 1:21; 2:36; 9:20; Romans 1:4; 1 Corinthians 1:9; Hebrews 4:14).

The crucifixion of Jesus was a very real event, witnessed by members of his own family, some of his followers, some of the ruling priests who mocked him, and by Roman soldiers who did the actual work of the execution. The crucifixion is referenced by almost every writer of the New Testament and by almost all writers, Christians or otherwise, who refer to Jesus. Only one person in antiquity denied that Jesus was crucified. He was an eccentric named Basilides who was active in the second century. He argued that Jesus played a trick on the Romans, so that they crucified the hapless Simon of Cyrene who helped Jesus carry the cross. The strangeness of this tradition and how it has been incorporated into the Qur'an and Islamic thought will be explored in a later chapter.

For now it is important to emphasize that the public activities—the preaching, teaching, and healing ministry—of Jesus came to a sudden and violent end with his execution in Jerusalem, either in the year AD 30 or 33. As it turned out, however, his death was not in fact the end of his movement. An event that Jesus had foretold, which his disciples scarcely could comprehend, happened early Sunday morning following his hasty burial. That event changed everything and gave birth to the Christian church. The movement that the Romans thought had been snuffed out was reborn and in three centuries swept the mighty Roman Empire.

CHAPTER 4

THE DEAD RISE

The Resurrection—A Game Changer

In a world where Zombies have never seemed more normal (not to mention popular) and the *Walking Dead* has invaded our culture through a record-breaking television series, it is difficult for the modern mind to appreciate how strange the concept of a resurrection was to the Roman mindset of the first century. The fascination of the dead rising has even captured the academy where it is now possible to earn university credit across the humanities and social sciences while enhancing one's knowledge of all things undead. Why stop there? The more zealous students can go on to earn PhDs because, according to a recent *Wall Street Journal* article, "It's clearly now acceptable to study zombies seriously."[1]

In our contemporary thinking, the dead rising is intriguing, even entertaining; however, in the world of Jesus the idea of a bodily resurrection was unheard of in Roman circles. Many New Testament readers fall into the trap of projecting their modern understanding of the world onto the first century. The world of Jesus and the early church was a world that is very different from our own. The danger is that if we do not know much about Jesus's world, then we will read our own western-culture modern world back into his world. After unwittingly modernizing Jesus and his world, a distorted picture of history emerges. Many don't realize they have done this, but that is what happens.

Romans of the first century viewed a physical body back to life from the dead as a disgusting thought for which, thanks to the pervasive influence of the platonic notion of the immortality of the soul, no civilized person would entertain or desire. The physical body was limiting, utterly useless. The influential thinker Socrates (c. 470–399 BC) held that one could become a star in the afterlife. The early church could not have chosen a more difficult place to begin than proclaiming their Savior, a condemned and killed criminal, had physically risen from the dead. The only reason the church professed and many died preaching a resurrection-centric faith was because *it actually happened.*

The Birthday of the Christian Church Was a Death

The popularity and influence of Jesus should have died with him, but it clearly did not. Absent of the belief in the bodily resurrection of Jesus, critics of Christianity have perhaps the most difficult problem explaining why there were any "Christians" in the first place (Acts 11:26: "at Antioch they were first called *Christianoi*," which means "Messiah-people"). After all, their leader was crucified as a criminal—considered empire-wide to be the most heinous and shameful way to die. Why associate a new movement with "that deceiver" (Matthew 27:63)? What caused the most entrenched opponents of the church, like Saul of Tarsus, to change course—"for to me to live is Christ and die is gain" (Philippians 1:21)—and ultimately give their lives for this condemned criminal?

The first century historian Josephus records the martyrdom of James, "the brother of Jesus" Ant. 20.9 and "pillar of the church" (Galatians 2:9). We know from the earliest Gospels that Jesus had at least four brothers—James, Joseph, Judas, and Simon—and "sisters" (Mark 6:3-4), and during his public ministry Jesus was an embarrassment to his family: "When his family heard it, they went out to seize him, for they were saying, 'He is out of his mind'" (Mark 3:21 ESV). Unreached family is something Jesus could identify with, "For even his brothers did not believe in him" (John 7:5). Why did James, like Paul, have this transformation and begin his epistle, "James, a servant of God and of the Lord Jesus Christ" (James 1:1)? The answer is Easter: "then [Jesus] appeared to James" (1 Corinthians 15:7). Two disciples were on their way home to Emmaus and told the traveling stranger with a note of defeat, "We had *hoped* that [Jesus] was the one to redeem Israel" (Luke 24:21), but their melancholy was changed to jubilation when they realized this stranger was the resurrected Jesus. Quickly they returned to Jerusalem reporting this appearance only to find the Jerusalem disciples also saying, "The Lord has risen indeed, and has appeared to Simon!" (Luke 24:34).

Belief in the bodily resurrection of Jesus was the driving force behind the growth and expansion of the early church from one hundred and twenty people in the upper room to a movement that by the time it had reached Greece in Thessalonica, the church had "turned the world upside down" (Acts 17:6). The Easter event overwhelmed the followers of Jesus to such an extent that it dominated their thought and became the very center of their preaching. We learn scared, scattered would-be ex-disciples of Jesus only fifty days after the crucifixion are united, unafraid, and bold: "But Peter, standing with the eleven, lifted up his voice..." (Acts 2:14) with the proclamation "this Jesus...you crucified and killed.... But God raised him up...because it was not possible for him to be held by it" (Acts 2:23-24).

The city of Jerusalem was teeming for the one-day celebration known in the Jewish calendar as the Feast of Weeks (Exodus 23:16, where on the fiftieth day [Pentecost in the Greek] following the Passover). Typically celebrated in May/June, the weather was accommodating for Jews to make the annual pilgrimage ascent to Jerusalem to offer their first fruits sacrifices (Leviticus 23:20). In Matthew 16:18 we hear the promise of Jesus, "on this rock I will build my church," which was fulfilled on the day of Pentecost in Acts 2 with the evidential proclamation, "This Jesus God raised up, and of that we all are (*pantes* in Greek: everyone) witnesses (*martyres* in the Greek: one who sees an event and reports what happened)" (Acts 2:32).

Luke's *incipt* (Latin for "here" or "it begins," which was the crucial opening sentence for an ancient book available only on a scroll without a "title page") in the book of Acts begins his report of the explosion of the Christian church around the Mediterranean, which clearly hinges on the resurrection event, with "[Jesus] presented *himself alive* to them after his suffering by many proofs (*tekmēriois* in Greek: verifiable event, evidence)" (Acts 1:3 ESV). The energy that united the apostles, launched the Christian church, and invaded the Roman Empire was the certain knowledge and belief that Jesus had physically risen from the dead.

Beyond a Reasonable Doubt

Our modern society and culture seems to revolve around weekend events. "How was your weekend?" "Have a great weekend!" "What did you do last weekend?" "Oh, our weekend was unbelievable." We have weekend trips, weekend brunches, weekend hikes, weekend sports, and social media is dominated—at times even littered—by weekend experiences memorialized in selfies. The most epic weekend of all-time occurred in AD 30, however. Dating based on Caiaphas's removal from office as high priest, as well as the annual Jewish Passover, we have a solid evidential basis to date the crucifixion of Jesus on Friday, April 7, AD 30.[2]

The forecast in Jerusalem would have called for warmer weather (temperatures being in the 70s in April). The city of Jerusalem would have been brimming over with Jews from all over the Holy Land who had descended on the city for the annual Passover festival. History tells us that something happened to Jesus on that first Sunday morning. Scared disciples are quite willing to die for what they had seen: "We cannot stop telling about everything we have seen and heard" (Acts 4:2 NLT).

Is it possible that what happened on an April day in Jerusalem could change the course of history and, more importantly, what impact if any does those events have on us today? How does the death and resurrection of a Jewish criminal affect me today? The bodily resurrection of Jesus Christ is at the heart of the Christian faith, so much so that if the Jesus did not rise from the dead, then "Christianity" would be nonexistent. Unfortunately, the most important fact of the Christian faith is also the most misunderstood. Most followers of Jesus have a woefully inadequate understanding of Jesus's resurrection. For many of our friends, Easter means nothing more than chocolate rabbits, painted and decorated eggs, and perhaps a corsage for Grandma.

Many growing up in the church have heard the resurrection referenced at Easter services and the occasional funeral, but often wonder, "How do I *know* that Jesus was raised from the dead?" Was this an educated guess on the part of the New Testament authors? What is the best evidence for the resurrection of Jesus? How can we know on critical grounds that Jesus's bodily resurrection is the best explanation for what occurred at that tomb in Jerusalem? Did the disciples steal the body? The salient issue of the faith is what happened during that epic April weekend. How we answer that question changes everything, especially how we live our lives today. The reason Christians for the past 2,000 years have proclaimed the resurrection of Jesus is because it is so well evidenced *beyond a reasonable doubt*.

The claim that Jesus was truly resurrected assumed a heavy burden of proof. Unlike any other religion, Christianity put itself to the historical test through explicit interaction with the Roman Empire of the first century. Many often miss this point. If these striking events took place, as the early Christian documents attest, then we ought to be able to find secular corroboration of said "Christian events." And there is secular historical evidence aplenty to substantiate the bold claims of the early Christian movement, claims that continue to change lives today.

History is a helpful asset for the Christian, which cannot be said for the Hindu or Muslim or Mormon. No other religion comes close to Christianity's interrelation with history. We have an overpoweringly attested source of materials in the biblical documents. For example, the Qur'an claims that Jesus was not crucified (4.158-58), only that he appeared to be crucified. This assertion flies in the face of one of—if not *the* most—definite fact(s) of antiquity: Jesus's death by Roman crucifixion. Jesus's death by crucifixion is unimpeachable. Are we to believe a seventh-century source about a first-century event, which contradicts earlier sources from the first, second, and third centuries? If we cannot be sure of Jesus's death by crucifixion, then we can be sure of nothing in history.

Why did Jesus's followers interpret his appearances in terms of resurrection? Appearances of Jesus would not in themselves necessarily lead to the conclusion that a resurrection had taken place. After all, Jewish speculation also entertained the possibility of post-mortem survival of the soul or spirit, quite apart from bodily resurrection. Moreover, Jewish tradition also allowed for ghostly apparitions—even the disciples on one occasion thought they had seen a spirit or ghost (Mark 6:49). So why did Jesus's followers speak of the resurrection of Jesus and not simply a vision of Jesus, or Jesus's angel or spirit? Jewish beliefs about resurrection envisioned a "standing up," which is the meaning of both the Hebrew and Greek words that are usually translated "resurrection" (as in 2 Maccabees 7:14; *Enoch* 102:8; *T. Judah* 25:1, 4; *T. Job* 4:9; *Life of Adam and Eve* 10:2; 41:2). Resurrection was assumed to be corporeal—physical (as in *Life of Adam and Eve* 13:3; *T. Abraham* B 7:16). Resurrection also implied exiting the tomb or place of burial (as in *Apoc. Ezek.* 1:1-2). Resurrection was, in effect, the reversal of burial. Unless these things could be said of Jesus, then his post-mortem appearances would likely have been explained in terms other than resurrection.

What persuaded Jesus's followers to speak of resurrection was their conviction that Jesus had died, had been buried in a known place, and had exited that place. These factors, in combination with the appearances, convinced his followers that Jesus was indeed the bodily resurrected Messiah. The resurrection narratives are found in all four Gospels, as well as the book of Acts (Mark 16:1-8, 9-20; Matthew 27:62–28:20; Luke 24:1-53; Acts 1:1-12; John 20–21). Every sermon in the book of Acts discusses at length or references the resurrection of Jesus. The book of Romans is regarded as the most important piece of literature in history—the most significant book every written. Martin Luther had his personal awakening that led to a reformation through his study of Romans.

In the opening verses of Romans, Paul gloriously states that Jesus was declared to be the Son of God with power by the resurrection of the dead (Romans 1:4). To the Philippians Paul said, "I want to know Christ and experience the mighty power that raised him from the dead" (Philippians 3:10 NLT). Over two dozen times—more than any other promise in the New Testament for the believer—is the promise that we will be raised with Jesus. The bodily resurrection of Jesus guarantees our future bodily resurrection. They are linked. Only because of the resurrection could Paul say to the Colossian church, "Christ in you, the hope of glory" (Colossians 1:27 ESV). Do you possess a resurrection-centric faith?

Unfortunately, most of the popular and critical discussion of the Gospel resurrection narratives suffers from a lack of adequate knowledge with Jewish traditions of death and burial, especially with respect to the burial of executed persons or persons who in some way died dishonorable deaths. It needs to be emphasized that in the Jewish world burial was absolutely necessary. Burial of all persons, including executed criminals, was to take place the day of death. No corpse was to be left unburied overnight, which was in part due to compassion, but it was primarily due to the scriptural command to avoid defilement of the land (Deuteronomy 21:22-23), a command observed in the time of Jesus (cf. 11QT 64:7-13a, where Deuteronomy 21:22-23 is interpreted in reference to crucifixion), and upheld in early rabbinic tradition (cf. *m. Sanh.* 6:4).

This tradition specifies that the executed person was not to be buried in the "burying-place of his fathers," but in one of the places reserved for the burial of criminals (*m. Sanh.* 6:5). The discussion concludes by recalling that after the flesh of the executed criminal had decomposed, his bones could then be gathered and taken to the family burial place, but no public lamentation was permitted (*m. Sanh.* 6:6). Josephus remarks: "Jews are so careful about funeral rites that even malefactors who have been sentenced to crucifixion are taken down and buried before sunset" (*Jewish Wars* 4.317). Roman authorities were expected to comply with Jewish customs, sometimes outside the land of Israel, as Philo attests (*Flaccus* 83) in reference to Roman authority in Egypt. In the time of the Roman governors (AD 6–66), the Jewish council lacked the authority to execute anyone. Because the Jewish council (or Sanhedrin) delivered Jesus to the Roman authorities for execution, it was incumbent upon it to arrange for proper burial (as in *m. Sanhedrin* 6:5).

Only during the time of insurrection and war did the Roman authorities not respect Jewish burial practices and sensitivities. For example, during the siege of Jerusalem (AD 69–70), General Titus crucified Jewish captives and fugitives opposite the walls of the city and left their bodies to rot in the sun to demoralize the rebels (*Jewish Wars* 5.289; 5.449). Titus did not permit burial, because he knew how important it was to the Jewish people.

In view of the data, it is probable that arrangements would have been made to bury Jesus and the other men crucified with him. Joseph of Arimathea, a member of the Jewish council, either volunteered or was assigned the task of seeing to the prompt and unceremonious burial of Jesus and, perhaps, the other two men who were crucified with him that day. According to law and custom, when the Jewish council (or Sanhedrin) condemned someone to death, by whatever means, it fell to the council to have that person buried. The Jewish council was responsible to oversee the proper burial of the executed individual because the bodies of the executed were normally not surrendered to family and friends.

Jesus was not buried honorably—no executed criminal was—but he was buried properly. Jewish law required it; and in peacetime Roman authority permitted it. All the details in the Gospel accounts of the burial of Jesus and the subsequent discovery of the empty tomb cohere with Jewish burial customs. The startling discovery of the empty tomb was a major factor in the interpretation of the appearances of Jesus in terms of resurrection.

A Skeptic Is the Earliest Source for the Resurrection of Jesus

The statement that Jesus rose from the dead "on the third day" is not restricted to the Gospels. In fact, it is found in one of the earliest Christian creedal statements in reference to Jesus's resurrection. Matthew, Mark, Luke, and John are careful to record the many "convincing proofs" (Acts 1:3 NET) evidencing the bodily resurrection of Jesus. Luke (1:4) said that it is possible for you to have a "certainty" about your Christian faith. The Gospel writers are excellent sources, but they are not the earliest sources for the resurrection of Jesus. This always surprises audiences. The best source, and by the best I mean earliest source for Jesus, is the former skeptic Saul, or Paul, the apostle.

The New Testament was originally written in Greek and there are 138,020 words in the Greek New Testament. Paul writes thirteen of the twenty-seven New Testament books and contributes 32,407 words, or 23 percent, of the New Testament. Only Luke with his two-part Luke–Acts series contributes more (approximately 28 percent) than Paul to the New Testament. Do you remember what Paul said was the most important point in his writings? In 1 Corinthians 15:3, the apostle Paul states that the issue of Jesus's bodily resurrection was a matter of "first importance." Indeed, Jesus's resurrection was the salient issue of the faith for Paul, and equally as vital in Christian origins. Paul is early, he gives us our earliest New Testament documents, and he is also an eyewitness of the resurrection of Jesus. Paul's letter to the church he founded at Corinth provides the earliest written witness of a Christian resurrection tradition and represents the oldest material in the New Testament:

> *For I delivered to you as of first importance what I also received: that Christ died for our sins in accordance with the scriptures, that he was buried, that he was raised on the third day in accordance with the scriptures* (1 Corinthians 15:3-4).

Similar to our modern recitals of the Pledge of Allegiance, the early church developed "creeds" or authoritative statements of what they believed and why. In the original language these "creeds" had a sort of cadence to them, they were poetic, and they could be sung and rhymed. The early church was creative in this way, and we mustn't forget the first century was an oral culture. The most important early Christian creed is found in First Corinthians 15:3-7, and there is no passage in the entire Bible that we should take more seriously.

Understanding this passage is key to understanding the theology of Paul and that of the entire New Testament. This early passage also answers the skeptic claim that the resurrection story of Jesus is a fable created in the years and decades after his death.

The villainous and psychotic emperor Nero (who reigned AD 54–68) martyrs the apostle Paul around AD 65 (Peter was also most likely martyred by Nero in AD 65). Nero's persecution of Christians begins in AD 64. This is an important datum because Paul would have obviously completed all of his epistles prior to his martyrdom. When does Paul write First Corinthians? It's actually fascinating because it is possible to date Paul's writing of First Corinthians with certainty to somewhere between AD 53–55. In fact, Paul writes to the church he founded in Corinth from Ephesus: "But I will stay in Ephesus until Pentecost," he tells them (1 Corinthians 16:8). Thanks to Luke's historical exactitude in the book of Acts, we learn that Paul first visits Corinth in Acts 18:1-2 to meet up with this dynamic Christian couple, who happen to share the same trade as Paul, Priscilla and Aquila, both of whom are tentmakers.

Aquila and Priscilla, being Jews, were expelled from Italy by the emperor Claudius (who reigned AD 41–54) in AD 49. In Acts 18, we learn that Paul spent eighteen months ministering and preaching in the city of Corinth. Beginning in Acts 18:12, it is clear that Paul makes an appearance for his "religious disturbance" before Gallio, the Roman proconsul of Greece (also known as Achaia). Luke's historical details are impeccable. Thanks to a profound archeological discovery with the name Junius Gallio incised at the Temple of Apollo in Delphi, we can pinpoint Gallio's term in office at Corinth to the year AD 51. Allowing enough time for Paul to complete what is known as his second missionary journey (Acts 18:22-23) would place Paul in Ephesus, where he writes to Corinth, in the year AD 53–55.

Therefore, Paul passes on an "early Christian creed" (1 Corinthians 15:3-5) to the Corinthian church in AD 53–55, which is the earliest gospel tradition or gospel message. It's known in scholarly circles as the *kerygma* (kay-rig'muh), "the message, or proclamation or preaching," which transliterates the Greek word (noun—κήρυγμα) *kerygma*—to preach aloud, to make a bold statement. This creed did not originate with Paul. Rather, we are confident it was in circulation before Paul because of his vocabulary use of "receiving" and "handing over" the information, which is very similar to the earlier and more formulaic communion traditions, also passed on by the apostle (1 Corinthians 11:23).[3] James D. G. Dunn is "entirely confident" in stating that the tradition lurking behind the composition of First Corinthians 15:3-4 "formulated as tradition within months of Jesus' death."[4]

The writings of Paul clarify *what* early Christians came to believe about the resurrection and also *when* they believed it. Paul is converted to Christianity in the early '30s or "about two years after the crucifixion of Jesus."[5] Then according to Galatians 1:18-19, Paul visited Jerusalem three years after his conversion on the road to Damascus: "Then after three years I went up to Jerusalem to visit Cephas, and remained with him fifteen days. But I saw none of the other apostles except James the Lord's brother." It is plausible that Paul received this early tradition from James and Peter within five years of the Easter event. What more can we ask for as students of history?

Paul's testimony is early and he is an eyewitness. Paul argues throughout his epistles that we have hope (in this life and beyond) because of the resurrection of Jesus. He is confident of this hope because he himself saw the resurrected Jesus and he was personally acquainted with many others, including Jesus's original followers, because they too had seen and spoken with the resurrected Jesus.

The Resurrection Can Be a Game Changer in Your Life Too

Allah desires that you die in his name (Qur'an 3:169-70; 9:39; 19:70-72); Yahweh died for you to have abundant life in his name (John 10:10). The resurrection is a game changer and proves that God is in the business of great comebacks. You might have lost your job—the resurrected Jesus can bring you a new beginning. Perhaps your marriage is in trouble—the resurrection shows us that God loves flawed, ordinary people. Perhaps you have experienced the loss of a loved one or child. Our family and closest friends who have died as followers of Jesus are more alive today than they ever were on earth.

Thanks to the resurrection of Jesus, Christians are promised that the best is yet to come and death is only the beginning, not the end.

This is why the apostle Paul tells the Thessalonian Christians who had lost their loved ones, "Yes, we grieve, we ache thinking about loved ones we've lost, but we do not grieve like those who have no hope" (1 Thessalonians 4:13 paraphrased) because the resurrection promises we will be reunited. The resurrection of Jesus is the harmonizing factor of life. Without the resurrection of Jesus, nothing makes sense. Thanks to the resurrection, we are promised no one is beyond the grace of God.

Paul sums up the true significance of Jesus's life, teaching, death, and resurrection in words that I find very helpful and insightful: "in Christ God was reconciling the world to himself, not counting (or regarding) their trespasses against them" (2 Corinthians 5:19). Note well that the essence of the life and ministry of Jesus was reconciliation (love, forgiveness, patience, etc.), not intolerance and hatred. No one is beyond the reach of God's grace, love, and forgiveness. It is our hope and prayer that you have met and embraced the living Christ and can say with us, "Christ in you, the hope of glory" (Colossians 1:27 ESV).

CHAPTER 5

WHAT ABOUT ONE'S ENEMIES?

Jesus and Muhammad Compared

Jesus was no ordinary Jewish man of the early first century. We don't say this as Christians; virtually everyone says this of him. What was it about Jesus that made him so different? What was it about him that throughout history makes most religions and many thinkers desire his endorsement? Why is it that about one third of the human race would like to think they are on good terms with this man of 2,000 years ago?

We could go on and on with these types of questions. Many sermons and poems have been written about Jesus of Nazareth. There is something about his teaching, something about his person, something about the way he lived, the way he died, and the way he impacted those around him and those generations who would later hear about him. More books have been written about Jesus than about anyone else in human history. He led no army, yet his unarmed following swept the Roman Empire in three centuries. Wherever his church has taken root and has grown, the human condition has benefited greatly.

Dangerous Minds

In popular parlance a "dangerous mind" is a mind that influences people and changes society. Many people want change; some don't. Jesus encountered people in Jerusalem who didn't want change, and Jesus died as a result. On the other hand, Muhammad encountered people who didn't want change, and they died. Both men believed in God. Both men recognized that society needed change. Both men had followers who were committed to their teaching, their vision, and their way of life. Yet the respective outcomes of these two religious teachers and their movements were very different. Why?

There are many reasons for the differences between Jesus of Nazareth, who lived in Israel in the early decades of the first century AD, and Muhammad, who lived in Arabia in the later decades of the sixth century and early seventh century AD. Perhaps the biggest difference is seen in their respective religious contexts. Jesus grew up in Israel, attended the synagogue, visited the great Jewish temple in Jerusalem, read or heard Israel's ancient Scriptures, and prayed. Muhammad grew up in paganism and polytheism, with some exposure to Judaism and Christianity. His was a world of tribalism, rivalries, and superstition. Unlike the Jewish world of Jesus, Muhammad did not stand in a long line of Scripture and story focused on the God of Israel and Israel's triumphs and defeats, periods of faithfulness and periods of faithlessness. Although there was, to be sure, variety in the religious world of Jesus, there was also stability. The God of the patriarchs was the God of David and his successors, and, of course, the God of the prophets. The result was a long line of stable theology and practice that was embodied in Scripture regarded by all Jews as sacred. Muhammad had none of this.

The advantage for Muhammad, of course, was that he had a very free hand to pick and choose whatever he desired. He respected the strict monotheism of the Jewish people of his time, so he rejected the Christian belief in the divinity of Jesus and the Trinitarian understanding of God. But Muhammad admired Jesus, accepted some of his teaching, rejected or modified other aspects of it, and was sharply critical of Jewish slanders directed against Jesus. Muhammad's teaching also included some of the superstitions and beliefs of his Arab upbringing, as well as some of the late apocryphal stories about Jesus. Muhammad's teaching is not limited to the Qur'an but is found in the Hadith (collections of reports of deeds and sayings of Muhammad) and in Ibn Ishaq's *Sirat Rasul Allah* (the biography of Muhammad), which in 1917 was translated into English.

Jesus stood in the tradition of the law of Moses, which included the covenant at Sinai, and, in effect, functioned as Israel's national constitution. Jesus accepted the authority of Moses but did not always accept how the law of Moses was interpreted and applied by the people of the day. Jesus embraced the prophets, believing (we may infer) that they consistently interpreted and applied the law of Moses the way it had been intended. He did not reject Moses or the Jewish faith, as is sometimes mistakenly thought. Rather, Jesus challenged his people to take to heart what the law and the prophets say and live in light of their teaching.

Jesus was fully aware that Israel's sacred Scriptures could be interpreted in self-serving and erroneous ways. This is why on one occasion he asked a Jewish expert in the law: "What is written in the law? How do you read?" (Luke 10:26). When Jesus asked this man, "How do you read?" he asked him how he interpreted Scripture. After all, because Israel's ancient narratives sometimes tell of battles and harsh judgments, one could interpret this to mean that God is a harsh and unfeeling judge and his people should behave this way toward outsiders or those who are regarded as sinners.

However, Jesus challenges this thinking in his well-known Sermon on the Mount (Matthew 5–7). In the first of several antitheses ("counter-statements") Jesus teaches, "You have heard that it was said to the men of old, 'You shall not kill; and whoever kills shall be liable to judgment.' But I say to you that every one who is angry with his brother shall be liable to judgment" (Matthew 5:21-22). Jesus does not disagree with the law of Moses, which teaches, "You shall not kill" (i.e., commit murder [Exodus 20:13]); rather, he challenges a very defective application of this commandment. That is, some people believed it was okay to hate someone, so long as one did not kill that person.

Consistent with this teaching is what Jesus says in another antithesis: "You have heard that it was said, 'An eye for an eye and a tooth for a tooth.' But I say to you, Do not resist one who is evil. But if any one strikes you on the right cheek, turn to him the other also" (Matthew 5:38-39). Once again, Jesus is not contradicting the law of Moses, for just compensation is expected (Exodus 21:24; Leviticus 24:20), but the law of Moses was not intended to justify retaliation or revenge. If one is insulted, do not return the insult. Instead, Jesus teaches his followers to "turn the other cheek."

This is again consistent with the point Jesus makes in the next antithesis: "You have heard that it was said, 'You shall love your neighbor and hate your enemy.' But I say to you, Love your enemies and pray for those who persecute you" (Matthew 5:43-44). For many of Jesus's contemporaries, this would have been a difficult teaching to adopt and live by. The Jewish people felt surrounded and sometimes harassed by hostile Gentiles, including their cousins, the Samaritan people, who lived between Judea in the south and Galilee in the north. One could find places in Israel's sacred Scripture where one could justify hatred toward enemies, perhaps even violence. But there are plenty of places in these same Scriptures that enjoin Israel to be charitable toward foreigners, even their enemies. So how should God's people read Scripture? That is the challenge that Jesus presents to his contemporaries.

Muhammad also challenged his contemporaries. However, his challenge was mostly focused on the question of monotheism. For Jesus that was not an issue—the Jewish people believed in one God, but the Arabs of Muhammad's time were mostly polytheists. Although Muhammad's preaching and evangelistic work began in a nonviolent way, in time it became increasingly coercive and militant. Here is where we see a great difference between Jesus and Muhammad.

PRIMARY SOURCES OF THE LIFE AND TEACHING OF JESUS (ALL FIRST CENTURY)

- The New Testament Gospels: Matthew, Mark, Luke, and John
- Quotations in the book of Acts
- Quotations and allusions in the letters of Paul
- Quotations in the book of Revelation

Enemy at the Gates

Jesus presupposed the validity of the law of Moses, often quoting it with approval. On one occasion, a scholar asked Jesus which commandment was the most important. Jesus replied, "The first is, 'Hear, O Israel: The Lord our God, the Lord is one; and you shall love the Lord your God with all your heart, and with all your soul, and with all your mind, and with all your strength.' The second is this, 'You shall love your neighbor as yourself.' There is no other commandment greater than these" (Mark 12:29-31). The man who queried Jesus heartily agreed with him.

Jesus quoted two commandments here. The first is from Deuteronomy 6:4-5, the famous *shema* (from the first word, *shema*, which means "hear"), and the second is from Leviticus 19:18, which commands Israelites to love their neighbors even as they love themselves.

All Jews agreed that it was paramount to love God with all that one is and has, but not all agreed as to the meaning of "neighbor." This point was raised in Jesus's well-known parable of the Good Samaritan (Luke 10:30-35), in which the Samaritan—not the Jewish priest or the Levite—was the one who cared for the wounded man lying on the side of the road and so treated him as a neighbor. The legal expert who asked Jesus's opinion agreed that the command to love one's neighbor as one's self was important. "But who is my neighbor?" he asked (Luke 10:29). When he finished the parable, Jesus asked the man, "Which of these three, do you think, proved neighbor to the man who fell among the robbers?" The man replied, "The one who showed mercy on him" (Luke 10:36-37). He was quite correct.

The beauty of the parable and the question and answer at the end is found in how the law of Moses has been interpreted. The legal expert's "who showed mercy" alludes to Deuteronomy 7, a passage that warned Israel to have no dealings with foreigners who will want to lead them astray by introducing idolatry. "Show them no mercy," Moses commanded (Deuteronomy 7:2, 16). Some Jewish interpreters in the time of Jesus and beyond interpreted that in a wooden and inflexible way. For them it meant never showing mercy to foreigners at all (whether or not the foreigners wanted to lead Israel astray). Some interpreters even applied the warning to Samaritans. Jesus knew this, and so did the legal expert who heard the parable. After hearing the parable he agreed with Jesus—even a Samaritan can be a neighbor, which in turn means the command to love one's neighbor includes the Samaritan. Jesus won the man over; he will never look at a Samaritan again in the same way.

It was this inclusive understanding of Leviticus 19:18 that undergirded Jesus's ethics and attitude toward people, whether Jewish or non-Jewish. Jesus rose above the parochial thinking of his day, the tribalism that viewed foreigners and outsiders as somehow having less value in the eyes of God. For Jesus, all humans are made in the image of God (Genesis 1:26); every life is precious in God's sight (Matthew 6:26). This is the way he read Scripture; this is the way he interpreted the law and the prophets; this is how he taught his followers.

But how did Muhammad regard enemies, unbelievers, and sinners (usually referring to apostates)? Muhammad viewed them very differently from the way Jesus regarded enemies. Let us compare some examples. We have seen that Jesus taught his disciples to turn the other cheek (Matthew 5:39); Muhammad was not so forgiving. He taught his disciples to inflict injury on those who have inflicted injury on them (Qur'an 2.194). In fact, in the Hadith we are told that Muhammad killed those who insulted him (*Sahih al-Bukhari* 56.369). Jesus of course agreed with the law of Moses that forbade theft (Matthew 19:18), but Muhammad permitted theft from unbelievers (*Sahih al-Bukhari* 44.668; Ibn Ishaq 764). Jesus agreed with the law of Moses that forbade murder and adultery (Matthew 5:21-26; 19:3-9), but Muhammad committed both murder and adultery (*Sahih al-Bukhari* 4.241; Ibn Ishaq 766).

Furthermore, Jesus taught his disciples to be truthful always (Matthew 5:33-37), while Muhammad permitted lying (*Sahih Muslim* 6303, *Sahih al-Bukhari* 49.857). Jesus blessed children (Mark 10:13-16), while Muhammad added a nine-year-old girl to his harem (*Sahih Muslim* 3309, *Sahih al-Bukhari* 58:236). Jesus forgave sinful women (Luke 7:36-50; John 8:3-11), while Muhammad ordered the murder of women (Ibn Ishaq 819, 995; *Sahih Muslim* 4206). Muhammad taught his followers to beat their wives if they were disobedient (Qur'an 4.34; *Sahih Muslim* 2127), but the followers of Jesus taught Christians to love their wives and be gentle with them (Colossians 3:19). Muslim men are permitted to rape female slaves (Qur'an 4.24; 23.5-6; 70.29-30), while the followers of Jesus are to treat slaves with kindness as though they are family (Ephesians 6:7-9; Philemon 10-20).

According to Jesus, God loves the world and wishes to redeem it (John 3:16). According to Muhammad, on the other hand, God does not love those who reject Islam (Qur'an 3.22; 22.38; 30.45).

Jesus blessed the meek and the peacemakers (Matthew 5:5, 9), while Muhammad promoted jihad and violence (Qur'an 8.39; 9.29, 111, 123; *Sahih Muslim* 4645). Jesus offered himself in service to others (Matthew 20:28), while Muhammad demanded to be served and owned or took slaves (Qur'an 8.41; *Sahih al-Bukhari* 47.743). Jesus willingly died by crucifixion (Matthew 27:27-50), while Muhammad believed that those who oppose Islam should be crucified (Qur'an 5.33; *Sahih Muslim* 4131).

Muhammad curses Christians and other non-Muslims (Qur'an 9.30), while Jesus's follower Paul taught Christians to "bless those who persecute you; bless and do not curse them" (Romans 12:14). Muhammad taught his followers to seize loot when they conquered and captured (Qur'an 48.20), but the followers of Jesus gave to those in need (Ephesians 4:28). After the death of Jesus his followers proclaimed him throughout the world without threats or violence, while Muhammad and his followers attacked countless cities and invaded country after country coercing the conquered to convert to Islam.

Children of a Lesser God

The God of Muhammad, whom he called Allah (a generic Semitic name for "God"), commands his followers: "O you who believe, do not take my enemy and your enemy for friends. Would you offer them love?" (Qur'an 60.1). Obviously this sentiment flies in the face of Jesus's command that his followers love their enemies, do good to those who hate them, and bless those who curse them (Luke 6:27-28).

Without question the difference between Jesus and Muhammad is profound, and the difference is ultimately due to very different understandings of who God is. In our view, the portrait of God in the Qur'an is largely Muhammad's projection, somewhat influenced by the monotheism of Judaism and Christianity, but deeply distorted by his own polytheistic culture, as well as by his own personality.

Evidence that Muhammad's vision of God was deeply defective is seen everywhere in Qur'anic teaching that pious and reasonable people simply cannot embrace. It is also seen in the bitter fruit that Islam has itself produced (which we shall review in the chapter 12). There is no question that Muhammad's monotheistic beliefs and his adoption of Jewish and Christian teachings represented an improvement over the polytheism and superstition of the Arab tribes of his day. But the hatred and bigotry, the violence and rapine, and the sexual excesses and barbaric behavior represent not the revelation of the God of Abraham, the great patriarch from whom the Arab peoples sprang, but a distorted image of a lesser god, a god who in some ways resembles the gods of the Ancient Near East, the gods who cared little about humans.

The Qur'an is itself the best evidence that Muhammad's vision of God is one of his own making. It does not derive from the God of Abraham, the heavenly Father to whom Jesus prayed and taught his disciples to do likewise. The God of the Christian Scriptures is much different.

CHAPTER 6

HIJACKING JESUS

What Muhammad Said about Jesus and the Jews

Muhammad (*c.* 570–632) greatly admired and respected Jesus. He agreed with Christians that Jesus was indeed born of the Virgin Mary, that he performed signs and wonders, and that he was a powerful prophet. But that was all that he was: a powerful prophet. The most important prophecy of Jesus the prophet was his prophecy of the coming of Ahmad, or Muhammad, who turned out to be an even greater prophet than himself.

Readers will wonder how it is that Muhammad, the self-styled early-seventh-century Arab prophet, could think of himself as even greater than Jesus Christ. Well, it is not clear that he really did; though many of his followers thought so. Indeed, most Muslims today think so too. But what made it possible for Muhammad or anyone else to be viewed as greater than Jesus was by *demoting Jesus.* Muhammad may well have thought that the birth of Jesus was miraculous, but he did not think that this made Jesus the Son of God.

Rejecting the Divinity of Jesus

Muhammad rejected the divinity of Jesus out of his zeal for monotheism, the belief that there is only one God. His understanding of monotheism was such that he could not embrace Christian monotheism that understood God as three persons in one, or what is known as the Trinity—the Father, the Son, and the Holy Spirit. The Trinitarian understanding of God (or the Godhead) is hinted at in Christian Scripture. After his resurrection, Jesus commands his disciples to preach the good news (or gospel), baptizing believers "in the name of the Father and of the Son and of the Holy Spirit" (Matthew 28:19). In the Gospel of John, Jesus tells his disciples, "I and the Father are one" (John 10:30) and "He who has seen me has seen the Father" (John 14:9). Jesus closely identifies himself with God the Father, but he does not claim to be the Father.

Other early Christian teachers use triadic language that clearly anticipates the Trinity. For example, Paul tells the Christians in the churches of the province of Galatia (in Asia Minor, today's Turkey), "Because you are sons, God has sent the Spirit of his Son into our hearts, crying, 'Abba! Father!'" (Galatians 4:6). Here Paul has referred to *God*, who is identified as the "Father," his *Son* (which in context is clearly Jesus), and his *Spirit*, that is, the Holy Spirit. In his very influential letter to the Christians of Rome, Paul affirms that Jesus was "designated (the) Son of God in power according to the Spirit of holiness by his resurrection from the dead" (Romans 1:4). The author of the Gospel of John speaks of the Logos, or the Word, who existed with God from the very beginning of time and, in fact, is God (John 1:1). At a point in time the Logos became flesh (i.e., human) and lived with people (John 1:14). Of course, the author of John is speaking of Jesus here. In some sense Jesus is God, but he is not the Father, nor is he the Holy Spirit.

It is from teachings such as these, and there are many more, that the early Christian theologians formulated what came to be called the doctrine of the Trinity. Perhaps the most famous expression of this doctrine is found in the Nicene Creed, which grew out of the great council that convened in AD 325 in Nicaea, in the province of Bithynia (in Asia Minor, middle of today's Turkey). We quote part of this Greek creed, which affirms the Trinitarian nature of God:

We believe
in one God, *Father* Almighty,
maker of all things visible and invisible;

and in one Lord, Jesus Christ, the *Son* of God, uniquely
begotten from the Father...

and in the *Holy Spirit*.

The Nicene Creed went a long way in settling important theological matters. But in the far eastern reaches of Christendom, the question of the Godhead was still debated and would continue to be debated for centuries. It is believed that Muhammad found himself in a context in Arabia in which Christians disputed among themselves certain aspects of the Trinity (e.g., in what sense Jesus was divine, how the Trinity should be understood), and in which Jews criticized the Trinity as a form of "tri-theism" (belief in three gods), asserting that Jesus had not been born of a virgin but out of wedlock. Aspects of the debate were obviously vulgar and insulting.

How much of Christianity Muhammad was exposed to is hard to say. He seems to have been familiar with some Christian beliefs and traditions, especially as they came to expression in eastern Syria in the second centuries and beyond. It is believed that Muhammad's wife's cousin was a Christian and so he might have learned some things from them. In places in the Qur'an it is clear that Muhammad, or at least the later compilers and editors of the Qur'an, was aware of Jewish beliefs and criticisms of Christianity.

Muhammad accepted Jewish monotheism but resented Jewish criticism of Jesus, especially the ugly insults. He admired Jesus and accepted much of his teaching, but he rejected the idea that Jesus was divine and therefore he also rejected the idea of the Trinity. In 610, at the age of forty, Muhammad began his mission, to convert his polytheistic Arab people, to chastise the Jews, and to correct the Christians. Along the way, he developed a long meditation, which after his death was compiled and divided more or less topically into one hundred and fourteen suras (beginning with the longest and ending with the shortest), known as the Qur'an. In this work Muhammad and those who compiled and perhaps supplemented his thoughts have much to say about Jesus.

Touched by an Angel

Muhammad seems to have been vaguely familiar with Luke's version of the birth of Jesus (Luke 1–2), or *Isa* as he is called in the Qur'an and Islamic tradition. Muhammad knows that the mother of Jesus is Mary and he seems to know, in addition to Luke, a version of the second-century legend of Mary's unusual birth and upbringing, which is recounted in an apocryphal work that circulated under various titles, such as the *Protevangelium of James* (i.e., the "first gospel" of James).

What we find in the Qur'an is a version of the story of the aged priest Zachariah (or Zechariah) and his wife, Elizabeth (Luke 1:8-23). While serving in the temple an angel appears to Zachariah and assures him that Elizabeth will give birth to a son and they will name him John. He finds this news hard to believe, given his and his wife's old age. The angel rebukes Zachariah for his lack of faith, telling him that he will be unable to speak until the child is born. When the priest comes out of the temple, he could not speak, but had to communicate by making signs. When his son finally arrives, Zachariah is able to speak, declaring that the boy's name is John (Luke 1:63).

What the Qur'an says about the birth of Jesus is also loosely based on Luke. Echoing the angelic annunciation found in Luke 1:26-38, the Qur'an tells us:

> "O Mary! Allah gives you good news with a word from him: His name will be Messiah Jesus, son of Mary.... He shall speak to the people when in the cradle and when of old age..." And she said, "My Lord, when shall there be a son (born) to me, since man has not touched me?" He said, "Even so, Allah creates what he pleases...." (Qur'an 3.45-47; cf. 19.20-22; 21.91)

In this interesting passage we read unmistakable allusions to Luke's account. These include allusions to the angel Gabriel's announcement to Mary ("Hail, O favored one"), to the effect that she will conceive and give birth to a son, whose name will be Jesus (Luke 1:28, 31), to Mary's puzzlement because she is a virgin (1:34), and to the angel's explanation of why this is happening (1:35). Of course, the version in the Qur'an says nothing about Jesus being recognized as the "Son of the Most High" and "Son of God," as in the angel's announcement in Luke 1:32 and 1:35, for Muhammad rejected the divinity of Jesus and the doctrine of the Trinity (Qur'an 4.171: "Say not 'Trinity'!"; cf. 5.17, 72, 75, 116; 9.30-31; 19.19, 88, 91-92). Nevertheless, Muhammad appears to have accepted most of the Christian tradition regarding the annunciation, the immaculate conception, the virgin birth, and the presentation of the youthful Jesus in the temple.

The next verse in the Qur'an is quite interesting. Allah will appoint Jesus to serve as "a messenger to the children of Israel." Jesus is to say to the Jewish people:

> I have come to you, with a sign from your Lord, in that I make for you out of clay, as it were, the figure of a bird, and breathe into it, and it becomes a bird by Allah's leave: And I heal those born blind, and the lepers, and I quicken the dead, by Allah's leave; and I declare to you what you

> eat, and what you store in your houses. Surely therein is a sign for you if you did believe. (Qur'an 3.49; cf. 5.110)

The story of making a bird out of clay and then breathing life into it is drawn from a story recounted in the *Infancy Gospel of Thomas* 2:1-5. According to this story the five-year-old Jesus is playing by a stream, forming pools of water and fashioning from the mud small birds. When rebuked for "working" on the Sabbath, Jesus "clapped his hands and cried to the sparrows, 'Be gone!' And the sparrows took flight and went off, chirping." His critics were astounded and reported to the authorities what Jesus had done.

Biblical scholars and historians do not think for one moment that there is any actual history behind this colorful story. Jesus's giving life to birds made of mud (or clay) is but one of several extraordinary (and utterly unhistorical) miracles the child Jesus is said to have performed in the *Infancy Gospel of Thomas* and in other related writings. It is on this very story that Qur'an 3.49 is based. This story appears in the so-called *Arabic Infancy Gospel*, which originated in the fifth or sixth century. The *Arabic Infancy Gospel* made use of the earlier *Protevangelium of James* and the *Infancy Gospel of Thomas* (see *Arab. Infan.* 46 for the story of the clay birds). It is probable that Muhammad was familiar with some of the infancy stories and perhaps had heard a version read of the *Arabic Infancy Gospel*.

According to the Qur'an, Jesus further claims, "I heal those born *blind*, and the *lepers*, and I quicken the *dead*." We again have a tradition that ultimately derives from the Gospel of Luke, for the Qur'an's words constitute an unmistakable allusion to Jesus's reply to John the Baptist: "Go and tell John what you have seen and heard: the *blind* receive their sight, the lame walk, *lepers* are cleansed, and the deaf hear, the *dead* are raised up, the poor have good news preached to them" (Luke 7:22; cf. Matthew 11:5). One will note that the Qur'an borrows three of the five elements found in Luke (the "deaf" and the "poor" have been omitted), in the order that Luke has presented them.

Rejecting the Teaching of Jesus

The Qur'an not only makes use of some of Jesus's teaching found in the first-century New Testament Gospels, as well as later questionable traditions found in the second- through fifth-century sources, but it sometimes has Jesus teaching things that contradict what he was remembered to have said in the much older sources. The preference for much later "revelations" that then trump earlier sources and evidences will be treated in the next chapter. But for now, it is important to underscore how different Jesus is in the Qur'an and in early post-Qur'an Islamic traditions.

What is odd in all of this is that Muhammad and the Qur'an do recognize Jesus as a great prophet. In short, Jesus is highly respected in the Islamic tradition. This is well and good, but it leaves us wondering how it is, if Jesus is such a respected prophet, his teaching is accepted here, rejected there, or altered somewhere else. Indeed, one wonders how it is that one prophet (i.e., Muhammad) can overturn the teaching of all preceding prophets (i.e., the great prophets of the Old Testament, as well as Jesus himself). After all, Muhammad was but a single man. Is it reasonable to think that his prophetic insight is beyond all that preceded him?

Muslims will say that Muhammad acquired his special knowledge from the angel Gabriel, who conveyed to him the words of Allah. Therefore, Muhammad has the final word. But the great prophets of the Old Testament also spoke the "word of the Lord." Indeed, most of the time they directly spoke the word of God without the mediation of an angel. In the case of Jesus, the angels themselves were at his command. As the glorious "Son of man" (Daniel 7:13) Jesus will "come with his angels in the glory of his Father, and then he will repay every man for what he has done" (Matthew 16:27). In the day of judgment, Jesus "will send out his angels with a loud trumpet call, and they will gather his elect from the four winds, from one end of heaven to the other" (Matthew 24:31).

These are *his* angels—that is, Jesus commands these angels. When in the wilderness tempted by Satan, angels came and ministered to Jesus (Matthew 4:11). Jesus later assures his disciples that if he wanted to he could request a legion of angels to come to his defense (Matthew 26:53). Should we accept the claim that the angel Gabriel conveyed to Muhammad new revelations that contradicted the teaching of the prophets and the teaching of Jesus, who possessed the authority to command the angels themselves? We don't think we should.

The Qur'an flat-out denies that Jesus is the Son of God: "Christ Jesus the son of Mary was (no more than) a Messenger of Allah, and His Word, which He bestowed on Mary, and a Spirit proceeding from Him: so believe in Allah and his Messengers. Say not 'Three." Desist: it will be better for you, for Allah is the only one that (God), Glory be to Him: (Far Exalted is He) above having a son" (Qur'an 4.171). What the Qur'an says here contradicts what Jesus himself says, when he stood before the Jewish high priest. Caiaphas asked Jesus, "Are you the Messiah, the Son of the Blessed?" (Mark 14:61, i.e., "Are you the Messiah, the Son of God?"). Jesus replies, "I am; and you will see the Son of man seated at the right hand of Power, and coming with the clouds of heaven" (Mark 14:62, i.e., "at the right hand of God"). Jesus clearly affirms that he is the Messiah, the very Son of God.

Condemning the Jews

Another unfortunate feature in the Qur'an, which appears often in contexts that speak of Jesus, is severe criticism, even condemnation, of the Jewish people. Again and again the Jewish people are cursed and disparaged in the Qur'an:

> Allah has cursed them on account of their unbelief. (2.88; 4.46)
>
> Allah is the enemy of the unbelievers. (2.98)
>
> On account of their breaking their covenant we cursed them. (5.13)
>
> They should be murdered or crucified or their hands and their feet should be cut off. (5.33) They shall have disgrace in this world, and they shall have a grievous chastisement in the hereafter. (5.41)
>
> O you who believe! do not take the Jews and the Christians for friends; they are friends of each other; and whoever among you takes them for a friend, then surely he is one of them. (5.51)
>
> Worse is he whom Allah has cursed and on whom brought His wrath, and of whom He made apes and pigs, and he who served Satan. (5.60; see also 2.65; 7.166)

Tragically many Muslims today still hold to these outrageous statements. Indeed, the claim that God has made the Jewish people "apes and pigs" appears in some schoolbooks in Muslim countries.

Muhammad is especially critical of the Jewish people in the passage concerned with the birth of Jesus. The Jews stand condemned, the Qur'an (at 4.156) says, "for their having uttered against Mary a grievous insult." Although the insult is not spelled out, it is probably the claim found in rabbinic literature, especially in the tractate known as the *Toledot Yeshu* (lit. "the Generations of Jesus"), to the effect that Mary conceived Jesus through adultery. For example, in the Talmud (where some of this material appears) we find: "She (Mary) who was the descendant of princes and governors played the harlot with carpenters (Joseph)" (*b. Sanh.* 106a).

The slander that Mary was an adulteress is what lies behind the habit of referring to Jesus as "Jesus ben Pantera" (as in the story of the man named Jacob who offered to heal someone "in the name of Jesus ben Pantera"). The sobriquet "ben Pantera" means "son of the panther." The Latin word for panther is *panthera*, which happened to be a popular name with Roman soldiers. We do not know the origin of the slur. It may have begun with Celsus, who authored an anti-Christian tract called *True Doctrine* (*c.* 170). Speaking of Mary, he says that "when she was pregnant she was turned out of doors by the carpenter to whom she had been betrothed, as having been guilty of adultery, and she bore a child to a certain soldier named Panthera" (according to Origen, *Against Celsus* 1.32).

Although we cannot be sure of the origin of the allegation that Jesus was conceived out of wedlock, there is little question that by the time of the second century, perhaps earlier, slanders against Mary and Jesus could be heard in both Jewish and pagan circles. Whatever its origin, the "ben Pantera" sobriquet suggested that Jesus was the illegitimate son of a Roman soldier with whom Mary had had a dalliance (or by whom she had been raped). What makes the sobriquet so delightful from a rabbinic perspective is that the Latin *panthera* may well have been understood as a wordplay on the Greek *parthenos*, which means "virgin." That is, Jesus was the son of the Virgin Mary all right —but not in the way you think! Muhammad found this slander highly offensive (and no doubt Christians did too) and spoke against it in 4.156. I think the Qur'an's reference to the Jewish insult to Mary sets up the criticism that follows in 4.157-58, which will be considered in the next chapter.

The Qur'an's traditions about Mary, the birth, and childhood of Jesus are based on limited acquaintance with the infancy narratives of the New Testament's Gospel of Luke (relating both to John the Baptist and to Jesus) and the fanciful infancy narratives found in the second-century apocryphal works *Protevangelium of James* and *Infancy Gospel of Thomas*. No properly trained historian views the latter two works as offering us factual history. It is unfortunate that Muhammad made use of their traditions.[1]

What we see here is the appropriation and adaptation of portions of the Bible's narratives. Although in this chapter we have focused on the story of Jesus, the Qur'an's appropriation of stories relating to Abraham, Moses, David, and other notable figures reveals similar distortions. The Bible's old stories are retold in such a way as to lionize the descendants of Abraham's son Ishmael (i.e., the Arab people) at the expense of the descendants of Abraham's son Isaac (i.e., the Jewish people). The stories and teachings of Jesus are retold, distorted, and supplemented in ways that transform Jesus into Muhammad's spokesman. In a sense, Jesus and the Bible have been hijacked and sent in a new direction.

Muslims, of course, will say that Muhammad has corrected the Bible and has presented the teachings of Jesus the way they should have been presented centuries earlier. Is the real Jesus reflected in the Qur'an? Should the Qur'an's seventh-century presentation of Jesus be preferred to the four first-century presentations we have in the New Testament Gospels of Matthew, Mark, Luke, and John? To these questions we turn in the next chapter.

CHAPTER 7

THE QUR'AN VS. THE GOSPELS

Who's Telling the Truth?

In the previous chapter we looked at examples where the Qur'an gives very different accounts of Jesus's teaching and life. In this chapter we will look at what the Qur'an says about the death of Jesus. Then we will turn to the big question that asks, who's telling the truth? The Qur'an and the Bible can't both be right. We begin with the death of Jesus, which, for the Christian, is hugely important.

The Death of Jesus in the Bible and in the Qur'an

Perhaps the most controversial element in the Qur'an, as it relates to Jesus, is the apparent denial of Jesus's death. For Christians the death of Jesus on a Roman cross is not only a given, but it is of vital theological importance. All four Gospels narrate the crucifixion, death, and burial of Jesus. Paul presupposes the crucifixion and death of Jesus throughout his letters, and the author of the book of Hebrews develops a major part of his theology in which he argues that the death of Jesus became the sacrifice that never needs to be repeated. The book of Revelation refers to Jesus as the "Lamb that was slain." Could all of these writers be wrong? Could the very disciples and family of Jesus have misunderstood or misrepresented what really happened to him? To these questions we now turn.

In the Qur'an (4.157-58) Muhammad rails against the Jewish people for boasting that they put Jesus to death. Muhammad was probably reacting to rabbinic tradition that claims that very thing. In the Talmud (sixth century), the authoritative compilation of Jewish law and lore, we read:

> On the eve of Passover they hanged Jesus the Nazarene. And a herald went out, in front of him, for forty days saying: "He is going to be stoned, because he practiced sorcery and enticed and led Israel astray. Anyone who knows anything in his favor, let him come and plead in his behalf." But, not having found anything in his favor, they hanged him on the eve of Passover. (*b. Sanh.* 43a)

By "hanging" one should understand crucifixion, in which a person was hanged on a cross until dead. The threat of being stoned reflects the Old Testament law that prescribed such punishment for idolaters and practitioners of black magic, even if they offered signs and miracles that seemingly supported their claims (Deuteronomy 13). This is what Jesus is accused of here: "he practiced magic and led Israel astray."

Muhammad was apparently familiar with these Jewish polemics. In the Qur'an we are told that Allah assured Jesus, "I restrained the children of Israel from (doing violence to) you when you showed them the clear signs, and the unbelievers among them said, 'This is nothing but magic'" (5.110; cf. 61.6: "This is sorcery!"). The charge of magic originated in the time of Jesus, as reported in all three of the Synoptic Gospels (Matthew 12:24; Mark 3:22; Luke 11:15), and was echoed in second-century pagan writers like Celsus as well.

Muhammad was very critical of the Jewish people for claiming that they had put to death Jesus. In 4.155-58, the Qur'an says:

> Allah set a seal upon them (the Jews) owing to their unbelief, so they shall not believe except a few…for they say: "Surely we have killed the Messiah, Jesus son of Mary, the apostle of Allah." Nay, they did not kill him, nor did they crucify him, but it was made to appear so to them. Those who argued this matter are uncertain; they have no knowledge about it except by speculation. In certainty they did not kill him, for Allah took him up to himself.

Although it is debated, the vast majority of Muslim laity and clerics understand this passage as saying that Jesus did not in fact die on the cross. The Qur'an explicitly and emphatically states that contrary to what the Jews claim, "they did not kill him, nor did they crucify him." It also states that it (Jesus's death) "was made to appear so to them." These words seem to mean that it only appeared to the Jews that Jesus had been crucified, but in reality he wasn't. But in what sense did Jesus only *appear* to have been crucified?

The appearance of the crucifixion, when in fact Jesus was not crucified, is clarified by the second-century debate instigated by one Basilides, a Gnostic heretic, who suggested that it was not Jesus who was crucified but Simon of Cyrene, the man who assisted Jesus with his cross (Mark 15:21). This strange hypothesis is sharply criticized by the influential church father Irenaeus (*c.* AD 180), who describes the view of Basilides as follows:

> He (Jesus) appeared, then, on earth as a man, to the nations of these powers, and worked miracles. Therefore he did not himself suffer death, but Simon, a certain

> man of Cyrene, being compelled, bore the cross in his stead; so that this latter being transfigured by him, that he might be thought to be Jesus, was crucified, through ignorance and error, while Jesus himself received the form of Simon, and, standing by, laughed at them. For since he was an incorporeal power...he ascended to him who sent him.... (*Against Heresies* 1.24.4)

Irenaeus's description of what Basilides taught coheres with the Qur'an's claims: It really wasn't Jesus who was crucified; it only seemed to be. Jesus (or an angel) transformed the hapless Simon to look like Jesus, while Jesus was transformed to look like Simon. Rather than dying on the cross, as everybody had thought, Jesus was taken up to God (which likely reflects the ascension; cf. Luke 24:50-53; Acts 1:9-12). It is to this debate between Basilides and Docetic Gnostics on the one hand and Irenaeus and the proto-orthodox Christians on the other that the Qur'an's references to uncertainty and speculation should be understood. Although Gnosticism as a serious threat had receded by the time of Muhammad (seventh century), some of its distinctive ideas lingered, especially in the East.

Whereas Basilides suggested that the man who was crucified was Simon of Cyrene, Islamic tradition came to believe that it was Judas Iscariot. Writing *c.* AD 995, 'Abd al-Jabbar (d. 1025), chief judge of Rayy (today's Teheran), claimed that through angelic intervention the "shape of Jesus was put upon Judas who had pointed him out, and they crucified him instead, supposing that he was Jesus. After three hours God took Jesus to himself and raised him up to heaven."[1] There is, however, absolutely no evidence before the time of Muhammad for the idea that Judas was crucified in the place of Jesus. But some Muslims think there is.

Muslims will sometimes appeal to a work called the *Gospel of Barnabas* for proof that Jesus really was not crucified, as the Qur'an seems to say. As we just noted in 'Abd al-Jabbar, so also in the *Gospel of Barnabas* it is the betrayer Judas Iscariot who is crucified (*Gos. Barn.* 220). As in the Qur'an's account, so in the *Gospel of Barnabas*, Jesus is taken up into heaven. But what of the discovery of the empty tomb, reported in all four of the Christian Gospels? According to the *Gospel of Barnabas*, some of Jesus's less enlightened and less spiritual disciples came by night and stole the body of Judas, thinking it was the body of Jesus. For this reason there arose the belief that Jesus had been crucified, buried, and resurrected. Muslims especially like the *Gospel of Barnabas* because in it Jesus teaches that the chosen line descends through Ishmael not Isaac (*Gos. Barn.* 43), denies that he is the Son of God (*Gos. Barn.* 53), and prophesies the coming of Muhammad (implicitly in *Gos. Barn.* 43; explicitly in *Gos. Barn.* 97, 163; cf. Qur'an 61.6, where Jesus shares the "good news of an apostle who will come after me, his name being Ahmad"[2]).

Historians do not take the *Gospel of Barnabas* seriously. They rightly recognize its lateness and its unreliability because of its many historical errors and anachronisms. These errors are numerous and for the most part quite obvious. Among these errors and anachronisms is the statement that Jesus was born during the administration of Pontius Pilate, governor of Judea and Samaria (AD 25–36). Not so. Jesus was born around 4 or 5 BC, shortly before the death of Herod the Great. The author of the *Gospel of Barnabas* describes Jesus as crossing the Sea of Galilee and landing at Nazareth (*Gos. Barn.* 20-21)! The author evidently does not know that Nazareth is several miles inland. There are many more blunders like these, as well as features that suggest this curious "gospel" was written in Europe no earlier than the fourteenth century. For this reason historians do not regard it as a helpful source in the study of Jesus.

The *Gospel of Barnabas* provides no historical confirmation for the claim that Jesus really did not die on the cross. On what basis, then, did Muhammad deny that Jesus died on the cross? All early sources—with no exception—claim that Jesus died on the cross. All four New Testament Gospels say he did. The apostle Paul, who wrote his letters to various Christian churches and leaders from the late 40s to the early 60s, frequently makes reference to the crucifixion or cross of Jesus. Other New Testament writings allude to it as well. It is probable that Muhammad denied the crucifixion of Jesus because of the assertion of Basilides and those who later repeated it and because he found repellent the Jewish boast of having killed Jesus.

However Muhammad came to think that Jesus really wasn't crucified, as all early sources say, we must ask, how realistic is this idea? After all, according to the Gospel of John, Mary the mother of Jesus was at the foot of the cross (John 19:25: "standing by the cross of Jesus were his mother, and his mother's sister...and Mary Magdalene"). What the fourth evangelist then narrates is quite important for our discussion:

> *When Jesus saw his mother, and the disciple whom he loved standing near, he said to his mother, "Woman, behold, your son!" Then he said to the disciple, "Behold, your mother!" And from that hour the disciple took her to his own home* (John 19:26-27).

Jesus has told his mother that she should now regard his disciple as her son and he has told his disciple that he should regard Mary as his mother. After that, the disciple "took her to his own home." If the Qur'an's version of events is correct, then it was Simon of Cyrene (or Judas Iscariot, if we follow the apocryphal *Gospel of Barnabas*) who spoke to Mary. Can we really believe that Mary had no idea that the man speaking to her from the cross was not her son? The whole idea is fantastic.

Killing History

We wish we could say that the destruction of antiquities by ISIS is only an aberration, something completely out of step with Islamic thinking and tendencies. But alas, it is not. Throughout history synagogues, churches, monasteries, convents, and the temples that belong to people of other faiths have been destroyed, vandalized, or converted into mosques in lands where Muslim armies have conquered. The Jewish and Christian populations in the Middle East, the very cradle of these ancient faiths, have been greatly reduced and in some places have been altogether wiped out. With the recent rise of ISIS, the world once again watches in disbelief as Muslim extremists kill and destroy.

Historically, Muslims have practiced a subtler form of violence against human culture: the destruction of history. It isn't enough to conquer lands, force people to convert, destroy churches, libraries, and museums; Muslims also rewrite history and, in effect, kill history. The biblical narratives of the Old Testament have been hijacked and redirected. The patriarchs and the prophets who spoke to Israel of God have, in the Qur'an and Islamic traditions, transformed themselves into "Muslims." The promises given to the patriarchs Isaac and Jacob and Jacob's sons have been redirected toward Ishmael and his descendants. Moses, David, Jesus, and others have become Muslims who support the teaching of Muhammad, even prophesying the coming of Muhammad. All the while the Moses, David, and Jesus in the Qur'an contradict the Moses, David, and Jesus in the Bible.

The fact that the literature of the Bible is many centuries older than the Qur'an doesn't matter to Muslims. And the fact that there is a great deal of archaeological and external historical support for the Bible's narratives doesn't matter to Muslims either. An angel spoke to Muhammad, Muslims believe what the angel said, and his words were written down as the Qur'an without error, the very word of God. *And, as such, all other source material—no matter how old, how close to the actual events, how connected to eyewitnesses—is of no importance.* The Qur'an trumps all. And why? Because Muhammad claimed he learned all of these things from an angel that conveyed to him the very words of God.

But how does anyone know that Muhammad heard and spoke the words of God? Because he says so? Because his followers say so? But what if it can be shown that some of what they believe is in fact not true, lacks support, and is contradicted by older and better evidence? Would not the failure to find support from corroborating evidence suggest that Muhammad's new revelation might not be based in divine revelation after all?

Of course, one must ask the same questions of the biblical narratives. How do we know if they are reliable and tell us what actually happened? Just because the biblical narratives are older and much closer to the times in which Abraham, Moses, David, and Jesus lived, does not necessarily mean they are any more accurate than the garbled accounts found in the Qur'an and other Islamic traditions. So why do many biblical scholars and historians believe the old biblical narratives are trustworthy and vastly superior to what is found in the Qur'an?

History and the New Testament Gospels

The New Testament Gospels of Matthew, Mark, Luke, and John are good candidates for telling us what Jesus really taught and did because they were written in the first century, the century in which Jesus lived, taught, and died on the cross. Three of the Gospels were written in the very generation in which the followers of Jesus lived. We believe that Jesus suffered crucifixion in either AD 30 or 33, and that the Gospels of Matthew, Mark, and Luke were written within thirty to forty years of his death. We also believe that the written sources that the Gospel writers used were in circulation many years earlier.

But the real reason historians have confidence in the reliability of the Gospels is that they consistently reflect the world of Jesus. In short, the Gospels exhibit what historians call verisimilitude, that is, they reflect *the way things really were* in the early decades of first-century Israel. The New Testament Gospels speak of real people, real places, and real events. They are such that archaeologists make use of them in determining where to dig and in interpreting what is unearthed. What archaeologist uses the Qur'an, especially in reference to ancient history, either with respect to the times of the Old Testament or with respect to the times of Jesus and the early church?

The New Testament Gospels enjoy corroboration from and correlation with archaeology. Cities and villages mentioned in the Gospels have been excavated. Archaeological finds clarify the narratives of the Gospels and the teachings of Jesus. None of this would be true if the Gospels were wildly inaccurate or fictitious. It is no wonder Christians pursue archaeology with such enthusiasm. Christians, Jews, and others (and that includes some Muslims, too, to be fair) pursue archaeology because it does correlate so well with the old biblical narratives.

Sometimes it is this correlation between archaeology and the Jewish–Christian Bible that leads some Muslims to obstruct the archaeological enterprise. Archaeological digs in Syria, for example, have been halted when it becomes known that what is being found corresponds with biblical narratives, not Islamic dogmas. This is one of the reasons the Muslim authorities who control the temple mount, where the Dome of the Rock stands (possibly on the very spot where once stood the Jewish temple), refuse to permit Christians and Jews to excavate on this holy site. If archaeological excavations are ever permitted, they likely would result in the unearthing of evidence that will support the biblical story of Jerusalem and her famous holy site, not the Islamic version.

Perhaps it is in part for this reason that ISIS thugs think nothing of destroying priceless antiquities and irreplaceable artifacts. They may wrap themselves in their banners of holy zeal for God, but what they are really doing is showing their ignorance and refusal to learn.

The same seems to apply in the study of ancient manuscripts. Unlike Christians and Jews who have preserved ancient manuscripts, which contain many variants and scribal errors, Muslim authorities destroyed Qur'an manuscripts that contained variants and scribal errors. Thinking they had eliminated the variants, they then declared that the Qur'an, unlike the Bible, was free from all error. Alas, but this is simply not true. Several Qur'an manuscripts survived and—you guessed it—they contain variant readings, scribal errors, and corrections. Unfortunately, because so many ancient Qur'anic manuscripts were destroyed, it will now be very, very difficult—perhaps even impossible—to reconstruct the original text.

Historians will always prefer sources that are close to the time of the events described. They will always prefer sources that are at least in part rooted in eyewitness testimony. They will always prefer sources that enjoy support, corroboration, and clarification from archaeology and other historical sources. And, of course, they will always prefer sources that exhibit verisimilitude, in that they reflect the realities of geography, topography, and all that is known of the places and peoples these sources are describing.

The New Testament Gospels are old sources that reach back to the time of the followers of Jesus. Furthermore, they correlate very positively with the finds of archaeology and exhibit verisimilitude. This is why historians and archaeologists (whether Christian or not) find them reliable sources. None of this can be said with regard to the Qur'an, which was written six hundred years after the time of Jesus, and contains no eyewitness testimony, enjoys no archaeological support, and exhibits no verisimilitude. The Qur'an exhibits the thought world of Muhammad and his closest followers. It gives us an argument about Jesus, but not the Jesus of history.

This chapter has touched on some of the negative things ISIS has been doing. In the chapters that follow we will take a closer look at ISIS aggression, strategies, propaganda, and eschatology.

CHAPTER 8

FROM CALIFORNIA TO THE CALIPHATE

The Wave of Westerners Joining the Islamic State

An astrophysics student from Turkey, a Briton with a computer programing degree, twin teenage schoolgirls from London, a hockey-loving young adult from Canada, and a rapper from southern California—these are the profiles of your modern-day fighter for the Islamic State, and they have all made the journey into Syria and Iraq to join ISIS. They are young, educated, connected, employed, born in the '80s and '90s, and drawn to the caliphate from the West.

According to the Islamic State, if you are a Muslim, you are already part of their caliphate, and your responsibility is to *hijara* (Arabic term for "emigrate") or enact jihad where you reside. There is no third option. In his first released message after declaring himself the caliph or successor, Abu Bakr al-Baghdadi pressed for emigration to the Islamic State, noting specifically the need for "people with military, administrative, and service expertise, and medical doctors and engineers of all different specializations and fields."[1]

In May 2015 the Islamic State released a thirty-five-minute audio message from the self-proclaimed caliph, al-Baghdadi, calling for global jihad: "O Muslims go to war everywhere. It is the duty of every Muslim.... Islam was never a religion of peace. Islam is the religion of fighting. No one should believe that the war we are waging is the war of the Islamic State. It is the war of all Muslims." No wonder Islamic wars are creating 10,000 refugees per day—a million Syrians fled for their lives in the past year while the Islamic State battled the Assad regime, evidencing an utter disregard for human dignity.[2] Even more concerning is the fact that ISIS messaging and virtual recruitment is gaining traction, if not a foothold, as more than 20,000 foreign fighters, male and female, have joined the caliphate.

Douglas McCain, an American citizen from San Diego, California, loved his family, basketball, Pizza Hut, and rap music. In 2004 Douglas converted to Islam and tweeted that his conversion "was the best thing that ever happened to me." Ten years later he died in Syria fighting for the Islamic State in August of 2014—the first American to die fighting for ISIS. Once described as a regular American kid, McCain was radicalized and lured to the Islamic State, dying not long after with his US passport and $800 in his possession. Identified by his neck tattoo, "Duale ThaslaveofAllah," his final tweet was, "Pray for ISIS." We mourn for Douglas's family. His sister Delecia wrote on her Facebook page, "I really don't understand why and how and I have no words, I never thought this will be the way we say goodbye."[3]

Jihadist Are Normal People Too

The Islamic State Al-Hayat Media Center (HMC) released an eleven-minute propaganda video entitled *The Chosen Few of Different Lands*, featuring twenty-something Canadian, Andre Poulin, of Ontario, now called Abu Muslim. With sophisticated graphics, professional editing, complete with a music bed, a boy-next-door looking Caucasian man appears on the screen sharing his personal testimony of joining the Islamic State. Andre draws attention to the fact he is a normal kid from Canada. He loves to watch hockey, enjoyed visiting the cottage in the summer, loved fishing and the outdoors, but he was a Kafir (unbeliever or infidel: the most terrible word in human language, according to Islam).

Even though Andre had money, a very supportive family, and good friends, he made the decision to leave the darkness and come to the light of Islam. He emphasizes that he was not some anarchist, hell-bent on destroying the world: "No, I was a regular person. And, mujahedeen are regular people too." A mujahid is someone engaged in holy war—jihad. As Andre is sharing his story, b-role appears of Canadian urban centers as well as serene landscapes. HMC closes the video with Abu Muslim (Andre) storming an airport only to be killed in an explosion. In the next frame graphic still photographs show Andre's deceased body and a North America voice-over begins quoting Sura 2.28: "Those who believed and those who suffered exile and fought (and strove and struggled) in the path of Allah, they have the hope of the Mercy of Allah: And Allah is Oft-forgiving, Most Merciful." The final scene is a dramatic clip of Andre highlighting the fact that he has only been a convert of Allah for six years. This video was believed to be the first Islamic State video featuring a North American. Al-Hayat would have us believe civilized westerners are joining the Islamic State and emigrating for Allah. The recruitment tactics appear to be working, especially through social media engagement.

In June of 2014 the Soufan Group released a study documenting a new generation of terrorists, with an average age of eighteen to twenty-nine (some as young as fifteen) were gestating in Syria. Over 12,000 foreign fighters from a minimum of eighty-one countries had joined Syria's civil war. By February of 2015, US intelligence stated one of their top terrorism concerns was the fact that 20,000 foreigners, 4,000 from Western nations, had joined the Islamic State. The breakdown according to the International Center for the Study of Radicalization and Political Violence is as follows:

Europe

- France: 1,200
- United Kingdom: 500–600
- Germany: 500–600
- Belgium: 440 (which is astounding given the population difference)
- Sweden: 150–180
- Denmark: 100–150
- Netherlands: 200–250

WESTERN EUROPE

Based on the fourteen countries for which reliable data is available, we estimate that the number of foreigners from Western European countries has risen to almost 4,000. This is nearly double the figure we presented in December 2013, and exceeds the latest estimates by European Union officials.

The largest European countries—France, the UK, and Germany—also produce the largest numbers of fighters. Relative to population size, the most heavily affected countries are Belgium, Denmark, and Sweden.

TABLE 1: WESTERN EUROPE		
COUNTRY	ESTIMATE	PER CAPITA*
Austria	100-150	17
Belgium	440	40
Denmark	100-150	27

TABLE 1: WESTERN EUROPE		
COUNTRY	ESTIMATE	PER CAPITA*
Finland	50-70	13
France	1,200	18
Germany	500-600	7.5
Ireland	30	7
Italy	80	1.5
Netherlands	200-250	14.5
Norway	60	12
Spain	50-100	2
Sweden	150-180	19
Switzerland	40	5
United Kingdom	500-600	9.5

*Up to, per million population.

REST OF THE WORLD

The estimated worldwide total is 20,730. This makes the conflict in Syria and Iraq the largest mobilization of foreign fighters in Muslim majority countries since 1945. It now surpasses the Afghanistan conflict in the 1980s, which is thought to have attracted up to 20,000 fighters.

With up to 11,000, the Middle East remains the dominant source of foreigners in the conflict. Another 3,000 were from countries of the former Soviet Union.

TABLE 2: REST OF THE WORLD	
COUNTRY	ESTIMATE
Afghanistan	50
Albania	90
Algeria	200
Australia	100-250
Bahrain	12
Bosnia	330

TABLE 2: REST OF THE WORLD	
COUNTRY	ESTIMATE
Canada	100
China	300
Egypt	360
Israel/Palest. Territories	120
Jordan	1,500
Kazakhstan	250
Kosovo	100–150
Kuwait	70
Kyrgyzstan	100
Lebanon	900
Libya	600
Macedonia	12
Morocco	1,500
New Zealand	6
Pakistan	500
Qatar	15
Russia	800–1,500
Saudi Arabia	1,500–2,500
Serbia	50–70
Somalia	70
Sudan	100
Tajikistan	190
Turkey	600
Turkmenistan	360
Tunisia	1,500–3,000
Ukraine	50
United Arab Emirates	15
United States of America	100
Uzbekistan	500
Yemen	110

Source: http://icsr.info/2015/01/foreign-fighter-total-syriairaq-now-exceeds-20000-surpasses-afghanistan-conflict-1980s/

The metrics for global jihad are sobering. According to the 2015 Munich Security Report, in 1993 there were less than 20,000 active jihadist fighters in the world. By 2013 that number had increased 500 percent, to 120,000 active jihadis. With the explosion of social media, that number more than doubled from 2011–2013 as there were less than 60,000 global jihadis in 2011. There are more than fifty Salafi-jihadist groups worldwide. The ICSRP released a thirty-day snapshot of global deaths due to jihad from November 1–30, 2014: 4,806 (2,206 in the Islamic State alone). According to the United Nations, nearly half (10.9 million) of the 22-million Syrians have been uprooted from their homes.

Jihadi John: The ISIS Poster Boy

Between August of 2014 and February of 2015, Jihadi John became a household name thanks to his central role in seven gruesome ISIS videos. Mohammed Emwazi, or now known as Jihadi John, graduated with a degree in computer programming from the University of Westminster in 2008. Born in Kuwait in 1988, Mohammed came to England when he was six years old, grew up in a middle class family in west London, and was known as a hard-working student at the Quintin Kynaston Community Academy.

That the centerpiece of brutal beheadings is a college-educated Briton has raised the flag on the problem of radicalization on British university campuses. According to the *Chronicle of Higher Education*, a recent graduate of Westminster University (Jihadi John's alma mater) wrote that their university was "unwittingly complicit in perpetuating such radicalization, as it has often allowed Islamist extremism to go unchallenged."[4] The *Chronicle*'s article "Britain's New Law Pushes Universities to Help Stanch the Flow of Islamic Fighters" noted a government estimate that between 1999 and 2009, 45 percent of those convicted in al-Qaeda-related terrorist offenses had attended university.

THE ISIS TOP TEN LIST

Over two hundred European women have joined ISIS to marry a jihadist. A Tumblr account attributed to Diary of a Muhajirah posted "10 Facts from the Islamic State that Everyone should Know":

1. We don't pay rent here. Houses are given for free.
2. We pay neither electric nor water bills.
3. We are given monthly groceries. Spaghetti, pasta, can foods, rice, eggs, and etc.
4. Monthly allowance is given not only to husband and wife (wives) but also for each child.
5. Medical checkup and medication are free—the Islamic State pays on behalf of you.
6. You can still survive even if you don't speak Arabic. You can find almost every race and nationality here.
7. For every newly married couple are given 700usd as a gift. (I'm not sure if it's still available now.)
8. You don't have to pay tax (if you're Muslim).
9. No one is conducting business during prayer time. You can see people left their shops opened and pray either in the masjid or nearby their shops.
10. The number of mixed marriages and mixed-race children are high. It's beautiful to witness brotherhood with no racism.

According to the Central Intelligence Agency, ISIS has a fighting force of nearly 32,000 across Iraq and Syria. The problem of foreign fighters joining ISIS is illustrated by the fact that there are twice as many British Muslims fighting for the Islamic State (1,500) than there are serving in the British armed forces (six hundred), according to Khalid Mahmood, a British Member of Parliament. The question is how and why?

How has the Islamic State managed to attract westerners by the thousands to join the caliphate? Why have young people left their homes and families? Well, we have American companies to thank for that, namely Facebook, Twitter, Tumblr, and Instagram. For all the positives we can list for our hyper-connected world, very unfortunately, the Islamic State has exploited the power of social networks and created a powerful platform that has brought terrorism into the twenty-first century; terrorism is now trending. We now turn to the unprecedented social media campaign ISIS deploys to lure western youth.

CHAPTER 9

TRENDING TERRORISM #ISIS

The Unprecedented ISIS Social Media Campaign to Lure Western Youth

Terrorism is trending on all social media platforms. ISIS has gone viral and the West is trying to regain lost ground in the virtual battle for the mind and heart. Even more remarkable than ISIS controlling a land area larger than the United Kingdom, over 35,000 square miles of Iraq and Syria (roughly the size of Maine or Indiana), is their digital footprint and influence, which has gone global. The Islamic super state is a lesson unequaled in unrivaled and increased terrorism brand awareness metrics: (i) social media engagement; (ii) web saturation, and (iii) content consumption and distribution. Young westerners continue to migrate to Iraq and Syria with their smartphone as their guide.

In 2015 the United States government initiated a process of hiring public relations marketing experts from the private sector *to put their creativity in combat to fighting an unprecedented ISIS propaganda machine.* ISIS produces and releases 90,000 messages every twenty-four hours through trans-media cross channeling. That is, on every available platform ISIS is present and entrenching its mission. Twitter, Facebook, YouTube, Vine, Instagram, Snapchat, Skype, kik, Whatsapp, Askme.com, ask.fm, commercials, films, and even video games are used by the Islamic State to sell their utopia Islamic dream—*and westerners are buying in.* "There's no question that what we're combating with ISIL's propaganda machine is something we have not seen before. It's something we need to do a lot more work on," said Jen Psaki, spokeswoman for the US State Department.[1] Well, actually, we have seen this before, albeit not on Twitter, Facebook, or the Internet.

> "Propaganda tries to force a doctrine on the whole people.... Propaganda works on the general public from the standpoint of an idea and makes them ripe for the victory of this idea."
>
> —Adolf Hitler, *Mein Kampf,* 1926

Aeschylus (525–456 BC), the "Father of Tragedy," famously said, "In war, truth is the first casualty." A *Mad Men* styled ad campaign gave one nation the confidence to attempt world domination, promoting a superior race while exterminating millions, believing the lies of one, Adolf Hitler. Hitler said, "The great masses of the people will more easily fall victims to a big lie than to a small one." Only days into his new role as Chancellor of Germany, one of Hitler's first acts as supreme leader was to established the Ministry for Popular Enlightenment and Propaganda. Joseph Goebbels was the mastermind who led the Nazi propaganda machine that utilized all forms of mid-twentieth-century media (cinemas, radio broadcasts, newspapers, publishing, and the arts). Every aspect of German life was idealized, even romanticized, on an epic scale. Nothing was overlooked. German life was superior to all else. In almost spiritual overtones, German media spread the message that the world needed to be Nazi and martyrdom was the central message. We know the rest of the story. After twelve years broadcasting the illusion of their superior race, Goebbels ultimately elected to have his six children poisoned to death by an SS doctor and then ordered an SS officer to shoot him and his wife to death on May 1, 1945.

> "He who wants to persuade should put his trust not in the right argument, but in the right word. The power of sound has always been greater than the power of sense."
>
> —Joseph Conrad, *Lord Jim*, 1900

ISIS in America

Don't speak Arabic? That's not a problem with the Islamic State. The "Anwar al-Awlaki Battalion" unit comprised of exclusively English-speaking jihadists within ISIS is dedicated to attacking English-speaking countries. In 2014 over one hundred and fifty Americans attempted to join ISIS and nearly all of them utilized social media to enhance their effort. James Comey, director of the FBI, called ISIS a "chaotic spider web" that continues to infiltrate Americans in the privacy of their own homes through unprecedented social media entrapment. This online enticement to radicalization has attracted men and women across the socio-economic-demographical spectrum and the FBI has cases pending in all fifty states of ISIS-supporters. John Carlin, head of the Justice Department's National Security division, says ISIS media is a battlefront for the hearts and minds of the American family: "They're [ISIS] trying to convince young people to go over and ultimately slaughter civilians in a vicious war."[2]

New America reported sixty-two individual cases involving residents of nineteen states who were at some stage of the process of joining or aiding the Islamic State. The average age of the sixty-two

Americans who have tried to join ISIS is twenty-five, with the youngest being a fifteen-year-old female—25 percent are teenagers. It is not possible to box in a profile for Americans wanting to engage in jihad. In fact, the only common denominator linking the group is their participation in the online world of ISIS. Representing a historical first in jihad, women are now joining the Holy War. Previous Holy Wars did not attract women to take up arms. But 20 percent of the Americans who have tried to join ISIS are women. As we have seen, ISIS is a misogynistic group that rapes, enslaves, and brutalizes women, so it is disturbing and puzzling to many that so many females are attracted to a group that is fundamentally anti-women.

Elton Simpson, originally from Illinois, and Nadir Soofi, a Texan, were roommates in Phoenix, Arizona, when they drove across two states to attempt an ISIS inspired mass shooting at a Muhammad cartoon contest in Garland, Texas. Elton's twitter account, @atawaakul "Sharia is Light," pledged loyalty to ISIS tweeting, "The bro with me and myself have given bay'ah to Amirul Mu'mineen. May Allah accept us as mujahideen. #Texasattack" in the moments before shots fired. Elton worked at a dentist office. Nadir was described as a wonderful father to his eight-year-old son and once helped save a neighbor who had collapsed with a heart condition.

Americans dedicated to the furtherance of the Islamic State were significantly influenced by jihadists' social media propaganda. Elton was communicating via Twitter with three ISIS supporters in the days preceding his failed attack. Twitter DM ("direct messaging") was the medium of choice to communicate plans for implementing the attack on American soil. Law enforcement is now faced with the daunting task of attempting to monitor the hive of social media activity pledged to jihad. There has been some mixed success. Twitter surveillance has led the FBI to thirty-nine arrests with ISIS links in over a dozen states. In the aftermath of the Garland attack, ISIS claimed responsibility and then proclaimed they have seventy-one trained militant fighters based in fifteen different states ready to carry out jihad. With the privacy and autonomy, not to mention ease, of a tweet or direct message, jihad happens. And the world watches and the tweets trend.

ISIS Selfie, Anyone? The Branding of Terrorism

The marriage of social media and extremism is an innovation. The importance of social media in the jihadi matrix has taken center stage. The act of terror is not enough; it must be documented and propagated on available channels. In 2008 ISIS created two Twitter accounts compared to 2014 when the regime created 11,902 Twitter handles. The Brookings Institute released a sixty-eight-page report, "The ISIS Twitter Census," documenting the pervasive online influence of the Islamic State, known best as ISIS, or ISIL, stating, "[ISIS] has exploited social media, most notoriously Twitter, to send its propaganda and messaging out to the world and to draw in people vulnerable to radicalization."[3] In a span of only eight weeks (October 4–November 27, 2014) the report noted no less than 46,000 Twitter accounts were advocating ISIS; however, there could be as many as 90,000 Twitter handles supporting ISIS. Seventy-three percent of the ISIS Twitter supporters use the language of Allah, while a growing number, 18 percent, use English, and 6 percent use French. Hashtag #ISIS was trending and its derivatives (in Arabic) were used 151,617 times as the hashtag of choice.

ISIS supporters are sending out over 133,000 tweets per day. They are on Twitter more than you are and they average more followers too. The average Twitter user has a little over two hundred followers while the average ISIS Twitter handle supporter has more than a thousand followers. ISIS has saturated the world with the convenience of a smartphone: 69 percent use Android, while 30 percent use iPhone.

ISIS media is multi-faceted, sophisticated, original, creative, and, from a technical quality standpoint, professional. Clearly, the Islamic

State has invested millions into their indoctrination world campaign. Similar to the Nazi Ministry for Popular Enlightenment and Propaganda, ISIS opened their branding office of communications, the Al-Hayat Media Center. Al-Hayat's capabilities rival any major Western production company as they seek to control the meta-narrative of the Islamic State. It's not all blood and guts either. Inspirational videos highlighting ISIS fighters visiting the injured in hospitals, AK-47 wielding females riding in exotic vehicles, a mujahid fighter stopping to eat a slice of pizza, and human-interest stories featuring the superior ISIS way are all dramatized with graphics and music.

Al-Hayat ISIS communications center, similar to the fictional media manipulation portrayed in the *Hunger Games* trilogy by the Capitol's domination of the twelve districts, preys on the vulnerable with savvy outreach methods. Therefore, ISIS, with cult-like messaging, has been able to attract supporters and fighters at unparalleled rates. CIA director John Brennan recently remarked, "What makes terrorism so difficult to fight is not just the ideology that fuels it or the tactics that enable it. The power of modern communication also plays a role. New technologies can help groups like ISIL coordinate operations, attract new recruits, disseminate propaganda and inspire sympathizers across the globe to act in their name."[4] ISIS is not beyond using children to disarm people emotionally to receive their message. They've dubbed their young boys "cubs of the caliphate." Accessing a Twitter video portraying child participation in an ISIS execution requires no more effort than downloading a song from iTunes.

You can be cool like an ISIS terrorist—or at least that is what the message is. No longer are we viewing haggard, camouflaged clad, al-Qaeda soldiers hiding in the mountains with less than stellar video quality. Interviewed on *Nightline*, Scott Talen, a social media expert and professor of Public and Strategic Communication at American University, described the excellence of ISIS' online footprint this way: "This is sophisticated. It is Madison Avenue meets documentary film making meets news channel with sensitivities and marketing value."[5] Talen points out that ISIS is speaking the language of youth, offering eye candy, moving images, cool music, graphics, all on demand. You can become a jihadist in the privacy of your bedroom accessing unlimited "how to" instructional manuals, along with emotional inspiration.

Jihadist hip-hop—who knew this would be a new musical genre? The gateway drug to allure would-be western ISIS terrorists is through hip-hop music, and ISIS video games with Call-of-Duty-like graphics and storylines. No need to hide in a cave in the middle of nowhere—one ISIS commander appears on an edited video encouraging women to join ISIS where they can live in luxurious homes and have stability. The message is they won't have that in the West. All the while the propaganda spreads, in reality ISIS is raping, sex trafficking, and enslaving its way across Iraq and Syria.

Countering the Virtual Caliphate

Unlike many churches and other social organizations, the Islamic State has a job for everyone. No one is too old or weak or marginalized to be important in expanding the caliphate. The message is that there is a place for everyone—*a place for you.* That message resonates with disconnected youth all over the world. We have over forty years of experiencing teaching in the university classroom and are often asked what surprises us about college students today. Without a doubt, we are saddened by the amount of baggage our university students carry with them to school. So many students are from broken homes. Many lack confidence. They have lost the security of belonging. The ISIS social media machine knows this and, therefore, their message is one of acceptance and belonging. No one is too far-gone to join ISIS. It hunts the outcasts of society. If you feel abandoned by your family, ISIS is happy to be your family.

The phenomenon of social media recruitment to terrorism is an innovation of the last five years. No longer is it necessary to go to elaborate measures to secretly join a terror cell, connect, and be radicalized in the shadows. You can join the virtual caliphate and in the privacy of your own home be resourced to enact terror all through the medium of social media. Terrorism expert Harvey Kushner says, "We haven't really adjusted. We don't really have a game plan. How do you infiltrate the mindset of this one or two or three radical individuals who are plotting something from the comforts of their living room couch?"[6] Counterterrorism officials are scrambling to respond to the ISIS social media deluge. The ISIS caliphate is digital and on demand, no longer secluded beyond vast oceans.

The CIA has for the first time in fifty years introduced a new directorate called the Directorate of Digital Innovation focusing on cyber world operations in counterterrorism. The Obama administration admitted that ISIS' digital influence has expanded across the social media spectrum at a much faster rate than the US has been able to curb it. The US Department of State announced the expansion of the Center for Strategic Counterterrorism Communications[7] (CSCC) under the new leadership of Rashad Hussain. Hussain is a Hafiz ("Guardian" in Arabic) of the Qur'an, having memorized it with the ability to recite all one hundred and fourteen suras of the six-hundred-page Arabic text. The chief aim of the CSCC is to magnify "prominent Muslim academics, community leaders and religious scholars who oppose the Islamic State...and who may have more credibility with ISIS' target audience of young men and women than the American government."[8]

The Forum for Promoting Peace in Muslim Societies has recognized its inability to reach youth and the fact that ISIS has intercepted and recast the message of Islam. At the Forum's 2015 conference, two dozen hackers were invited to participate in the program with one of the conference organizers asserting the need to speak the language of youth in the virtual world.[9]

Notwithstanding these efforts, there is a deeper spiritual issue in play. The Islamic State is capitalizing on the broken homes of the West and broken promises of Hollywood. There are more ways to connect and be connected and yet young people have never felt more isolated. The gospel of Jesus Christ promises that the kingdom of God is coming to earth and has started through us. If you know Christ, then you are part of God's kingdom. God has a plan for you, and no one is left out—all are welcome.

At the very center of Jesus's proclamation is the kingdom of God. Indeed, the kingdom of God is itself the gospel or good news for which Israel has waited: "The time is fulfilled, and the kingdom of God is at hand; repent, and believe in the gospel" (Mark 1:15). The kingdom of Jesus was foretold in Isaiah 61:1-2:

> *The Spirit of the Lord God is upon me, because the Lord has anointed me to bring good news to the poor; he has sent me to bind up the brokenhearted, to proclaim liberty to the captives, and the opening of the prison to those who are bound; to proclaim the year of the Lord's favor* (ESV).

Good news to the poor, healing the brokenhearted, liberty to captives, freedom for all in Christ. Human beings are spiritual beings. We hunger for the spiritual. And only Jesus Christ can meet the spiritual need we all have and bring lasting peace and purpose to our lives. This is the message of Jesus. Listen to it. The message of jihad enslaves, but the message of Jesus liberates. That message has resonated (dare we say, trended) for the last 2,000 years.

CHAPTER 10

THE ISIS ENDGAME

Dabiq and Jesus's Islamic Second Coming

It is not necessary to speculate or guess at what the endgame is for the Islamic State. In fact, to make certain the world is not confused about its fascistic ambitions, the Islamic State publishes a polished, idealized, and romanticized propaganda magazine called *Dabiq*. Only two weeks after Abu Bakr al-Baghdadi proclaimed himself the rightful eighth caliph, the first issue of *Dabiq* appeared in numerous languages, including English. The official magazine of the Islamic State is a psychotic conflation resembling a train wreck of *Sports Illustrated* meets *Mein Kampf* with the graphic brutality of a *Walking Dead* comic (with gruesome images) sprinkled with passages from the Qur'an and Hadith.

Most of *Dabiq's* twenty-six-page first issue is dedicated to the declaration of the "Khilafah" (which is the transliteration of the Arabic ةفالخ or caliphate) under the header of "Breaking News: A New Era Has Arrived of Might and Dignity for the Muslims," accented by this excerpt: "On the first of Ramadan 1435H, the revival of the Khilafah was announced by the spokesman for the Islamic State, Shaykh Abu Muhammad al-'Adanani ash-Shami." ISIS does not hide the fact that their vision of a new world order is the genocide of Christians, Jews, and any other Kafir (unbelievers) for the purpose of purifying the world.

Can you imagine a world without Christians? The ISIS utopia does not include freedom of thought, freedom of expression, freedom of speech, freedom of religion, or freedom to choose. Did you know that Jesus is mentioned on more than one occasion in the first issue of *Dabiq*? Dabiq is an essential component to Islamic State eschatology (matters of the end times) both theologically and geographically. It is a location (in northern Syria, six miles south of the Turkish border), but it is also an event, what you might refer to as the "Islamic Armageddon." This explains why the Islamic State was intent on overtaking the small town of less than 4,000 inhabitants. In fact, "Armageddon" is mentioned in the first issue of *Dabiq*, so establishing the context is essential to understanding their endgame.

When we lead tours to the Holy Land, one of the most fascinating sites in all Israel is Megiddo. This site controlled the best passageway through the Carmel/Gilboa mountain range and the Esdraelon/Jezreel/Megiddo Valley. The fortress at Megiddo was built to guard the Megiddo pass and it was at this site and in the surrounding territories that many historic battles were fought. Megiddo was the location where: (i) Sisera was slain during the period of the judges, (ii) Solomon and later Ahab built military outposts with chariots and horses, (iii) King Josiah was slain by Pharaoh Necho, (iv) Napoleon rescued his horsemen in AD 1799, (v) and it was also here that General Allenby defeated the Ottomans in a great battle during World War I. Finally, according to Christian eschatology, Megiddo is the location of the world's last battle, and that is why it is called the battle of "Armageddon," which literally means "the battle at the hill of Megiddo." It is a comparative oversimplification and one that certainly needs to be nuanced, but for our survey here Dabiq is for Islam what Megiddo is for Christianity.

The centerfold (pages 4–5) of *Dabiq* casts the significance of its name by an extended quotation from the Hadith, of which Jesus Christ (mentioned three times), or Isa as he is known in the Qur'an, plays a central role. Dabiq is heralded as a beacon and its geographical importance is underscored as the location of "one of the greatest battles between the Muslims and the crusaders." It utilizes symbolic language often referring to the "crusaders," "Constantinople," and "Rome." Then in bold, gold typeset is the Hadith promise that from Dabiq Muslims will conquer the world:

> Abu Huraira reported Allah's Messenger (may peace be upon him) as saying: The Last Hour would not come until the Romans would land at al-A'maq or in Dabiq. An army consisting of the best (soldiers) of the people of the earth at that time will come from Medina (to counteract them). When they will arrange themselves in ranks, the Romans would say: Do not stand between us and those (Muslims) who took prisoners from amongst us. Let us fight with them; and the Muslims would say: Nay, by Allah, we would never get aside from you and from our brethren that you may fight them. They will then fight and a third (part) of the army would run away, whom Allah will never forgive. A third (part of the army), which would be constituted of excellent martyrs in Allah's eye, would be killed and the third who would never be put to trial would win and they would be conquerors of Constantinople. And as they would be busy in distributing the spoils of war (amongst themselves) after hanging their swords by the olive trees, the Satan would cry: The Dajjal has taken your place among your family. They would then come out, but it would

> be of no avail. And when they would come to Syria, he would come out while they would be still preparing themselves for battle drawing up the ranks. Certainly, the time of prayer shall come and then Jesus (peace be upon him) son of Mary would descend and would lead them in prayer. When the enemy of Allah would see him, it would (disappear) just as the salt dissolves itself in water and if he (Jesus) were not to confront them at all, even then it would dissolve completely, but Allah would kill them by his hand and he would show them their blood on his lance (the lance of Jesus Christ). (Sahih Muslim 41.6924)

In the second issue of *Dabiq* is an illustration of Noah's ark and the great flood: "It's either the Islamic State or the Flood." In other words, you join the Islamic State or you will be destroyed. There is no middle ground. Anyone—political leader, a religious cleric, or a soccer mom—who claims that the Islamic State is un-Islamic, is only flaunting his or her ignorance. The silver lining of each issue of *Dabiq* is passages from the Qur'an and Hadith promising victory in war, blessings in this life and the life to come, complete with exegetical studies. For example, part three of the second issue is titled "Contemplating the Verses," and it is a polemic against pacifism and allowing people a choice of worshiping Allah.

Break Your Crosses and Enslave Your Women, by the Permission of Allah

Every issue of *Dabiq* is appalling and apocalyptic, and always cryptic; however, each new issue appears to outdo the previous with an ever-increasing amount of vile images. Dismembered corpses, dead babies and children, all at the hands of the western crusaders—nothing is off-limits. The cover of issue four of *Dabiq* features the Black Standard of the Islamic State pinned to the top of the sixteenth-century Egyptian obelisk at the center of St. Peter's Square in Vatican City. The imperialistic overtones are clear: the Islamic State will conquer Rome and cover the earth. This issue is dedicated to the theme "The Failed Crusade" and depicts caskets draped with the American flag with the following statement: "We will conquer your Rome, break your crosses, and enslave your women, by the permission of Allah, the Exalted. This is His promise. If we do not reach that time, then our children and grandchildren will reach it, and they will sell your sons as slaves at the slave market." Indeed, citing a prophecy by Muhammad, this issue of *Dabiq* is an Islamic State advancement of slavery and human trafficking "that the slave girl gives birth to her master," as a sign of the end times. ISIS takes credit for a "large-scale enslavement" of the Yazidis, who are "now sold by the Islamic State soldiers."

THE BLACK STANDARD OF THE ISLAMIC STATE AND JESUS THE KILLER

The Black Standard of the Islamic State looks back and forward with significance. Looking back, the black flag memorializes the eighth-century Umayyad caliphate dynasty who, while wielding the black flags of Islam, reigned over 5 million square miles, one of the largest contiguous empires to ever exist. Looking forward, ISIL's black flag is eschatological and symbolic of the final battles to be fought at the end of time with the Muslim savior known as the Mahdi. The white letters are the first phrase of the *shahada: "La ilah illa llah"* ("there is no god but Allah" [*Sura* 2:255; 28:88; 112:1-4]). The black letters inside the circle complete the *shahada: "Wa Muhammadu rasul u'llah"* ("and Muhammad is Allah's messenger" [*Sura* 33:40; 48:29; 64:8]).

According to Muslim traditions, a descendant of Muhammad, an Islamic-superman (Messiah), known as the Mahdi, will emerge at the end of days and rule the world with a group of warriors wielding black flags. Jesus will return in his second coming to serve the Mahdhi. In his second coming, Jesus is the ultimate Muslim, a great warrior, and will lead the world in Sharia with an iron fist. Jesus will appear as Muslims face annihilation at the hands of the anti-Muslim, anti-Messiah figure known as the Dajjal. He will kill the Dajjal and save the Muslim faith. Then he will break the crosses, end Christianity (and abolish the jizya tax since non-Muslims will no longer exist), kill all of the pigs, make the hajj (pilgrimage) to Mecca, marry, have children, and eventually die. Muhammad enlightens us on Jesus's appearance—he is a man of medium stature, somewhere between red and white, and looks like he is dripping wet, similar to a Chanel cologne commercial.

Allah's apostle said, "The Hour will not be established until the son of Mary (i.e. Jesus) descends amongst you as a just ruler, he will break the cross, kill the pigs, and abolish the Jizya tax. Money will be in abundance so that nobody will accept it (as charitable gifts)" (Bukhari 3.43.656).

> The Prophet (peace be upon him) said: There is no prophet between me and him, that is, Jesus (peace be upon him). He will descend (to the earth). When you see him, recognise him: a man of medium height, reddish

> fair, wearing two light yellow garments, looking as if drops were falling down from his head though it will not be wet. He will fight the people for the cause of Islam. He will break the cross, kill swine, and abolish jizyah. Allah will perish all religions except Islam. He will destroy the Antichrist and will live on the earth for forty years and then he will die. The Muslims will pray over him. (Abu Dawud 37.4310)

According to Islam, Jesus is not the Son of God, he was not resurrected, and he is not a Savior. Even so, he is the second most revered prophet, after Muhammad of course. He did in fact have a miraculous birth, born of a virgin, and rather than dying on a Roman cross, he was translated to heaven much like Enoch, thus escaping death. Therefore, Jesus is now physically in heaven and can return to earth at the appointed hour. "But they killed him not, nor crucified him; It was only a likeness shown to them: Most certainly they killed him not. Rather, God lifted him up to Himself" (Qur'an 4:157-8). According to Islamic traditions, Jesus does not return to save the world, but rather to slaughter all those who do not embrace Islam. Jesus will return in Syria, to the east of Damascus, and not in Jerusalem on the Mount of Olives as the Bible predicts.

The Islamic State in a Machiavellian fashion uses the power of the printed page to recruit westerners to join the caliphate. Over 20,000 foreign fighters have emigrated to Syria and Iraq, answering the call of the Abu Bakr al-Baghdadi. Most Christians are woefully unaware that their Jesus, or Isa, plays a central role in establishing Islam for all in the end times.

The picture and message of Jesus found in the New Testament is urgently needed today. The message of Jesus is about God's love for *all* humanity. The message of Christianity is unique and the best-known Bible verse begins with the words, "For God so loved the world..." (John 3:16). Jesus's message is one of love, reconciliation, redemption, and transformation. It is a message of forgiveness and hope, a message that brings humans together and brings them into a loving and joyous relationship with God, the Creator of the universe, a message that resonates in the hearts of its hearers. The message of the Bible stands in stark contrast with the messages of those who think God no longer has anything to offer or that Christian faith is passé. The Bible speaks compellingly of God's love for humanity—*all humanity*—in an eternal relationship.

CHAPTER 11

REFORMING ISLAM, THE CULT OF DEATH

Women in Islam and Ayaan Hirsi Ali—the Reformer

"Let's stop going after Christians and Christianity. Let's go after Islam as the most threatening doctrine of our time. Let's ask them those questions that we put to the other religions," were the closing words Ayaan Hirsi Ali spoke, an ex-Muslim turned atheist, and the keynote speaker at the 2015 National American Atheist Convention in Memphis, Tennessee. As fate would have it, our organization happened to be present for Ayaan's presentation. We lead a nonprofit 501(c)3 called Christian Thinkers Society (CTS), and our mission is to inspire "Christians to become thinkers and thinkers to become Christians." Had not our launch director, CTS team, and film crew been present on April 3, 2015, conducting interviews and filming at the keynote session at the atheist convention, we're not sure we would have expected to hear such an articulate polemic against global Islamic extremism, the Qur'an, and the Islamic State of Iraq and Syria.

Our purpose was to film with many atheists and ask the "why" question. Why had many of them left Christianity for atheism? Several answers were offered. One atheist, a former Catholic, became an atheist in his Old Testament class at divinity school, not understanding aspects of the Old Testament. Another atheist, a former Southern Baptist, said that the lack of critical thinking skills drove him to question everything about his faith.

Two reasons enforcing their entrenched atheism were offered in almost every interview: suffering in the world and the lack of critical thinking are the main arguments undergirding their atheism. As often is the case when filming, unexpected nuggets emerge that enhance the overall project. Ayaan Hirsi Ali's keynote address at the Peabody Hotel was a watershed moment as she drew a line in the sand and said Islam must be reformed.

Not All Religions Are the Same

Ayaan's story of survival is moving. In her early twenties, Ayaan Hirsi Ali, born in Mogadishu, Somalia, escaped an arranged marriage and fled to the Netherlands, leaving behind her family and ultimately her faith in Islam. As a child, Ayaan was subjected to female genital mutilation, rigid adherence to Islam, and she began questioning the faith of her upbringing. After her escape and experience of being disowned by her family, all alone Ayaan worked as a maid cleaning factories in the Netherlands and learned Dutch. Eventually, she graduated with a degree in political science from Leiden University in 2000 and began speaking out about the abuses of women within Islam.

Four years after graduating, Ayaan wrote the screenplay for *Submission*, a short film directed by Theo van Goh (1957–2004), about the horrors of Islamic mistreatment of women. Less than three months after the film aired on Dutch public television, van Goh was brutally murdered (shot, stabbed, and mutilated after an unsuccessful attempt at beheading) on a public street in Amsterdam. His assailant, Mohammed Bouyeri, left a cryptic note harpooned to Mr. van Goh's body threatening the life of Ayaan Hirsi Ali. Since 2004 Ayaan has lived under constant threat and requires a constant security detail. In 2005, she was named one of *Time Magazine's* 100 Most Influential People and in 2013 became a United States citizen. Ayaan, now an ardent atheist, serves as a Fellow at the Harvard Kennedy School and is a best-selling author and courageously decries the threat of Islam on civilization as we know it. Ayaan hopes to be for Islam what Martin Luther was for Christianity—a reformer.

Ayaan made some courageous and powerful statements for her colleagues at the National American Atheist Convention. First, not all religions are the same she said. She drew a contrast between Islam and Christianity by stating that the worst thing that will happen to you if you leave Christianity is that you may end up divorced or your neighbors may disown you; however, leaving Islam is a death sentence. Given the collective limited time and resources of the American Atheists, Ayaan's passionate plea was to focus on the far greater threat of Islam. Ayaan will never come to terms with the fact that Muslims all over the world want to kill her for leaving Islam; and not only her, but anyone who doubts the Qur'an or Muhammad are subjected to persecution and risks death. Ayaan contrasts the reality that if you are gay in the United States, the worst thing the Christian community can do to you is not serve you cake; however, if you are gay, or simply accused of being gay in Islam, you are led to the highest point of your local town (building or hill) and thrown off the precipice where an angry mob waits for you on the ground for stoning (if by chance one survives the fall). The Hadith commands, "If a man who is not married is seized committing sodomy, he will be stoned to death" (Abu Dawud 4448).

> The Prophet cursed effeminate men (those men who are in the similitude [assume the manners] of women) and those women who assume the manners of men, and he said, "Turn them out of your houses." The Prophet turned out such-and-such man, and 'Umar turned out such-and-such woman. (Bukhari 72.774)

Ayaan applauds the fact that Christians are committed to critical thinking, discussion, and engagement, unlike Muslims. Islam is the religion of discrimination and the cult of death. Ayaan is an apologist defending the freedom of conscience for all humanity. People should be free to worship as they choose or not worship at all. In an Islamic society, religious freedom does not exist. If you are a woman in Islam, you are already in hell. You are a slave. You have no rights. If you are raped or abused, it is your own fault. According to Ayaan, Islam incubates the worst level of segregation we have ever seen. She quotes Voltaire (although the actual quote comes from Evelyn Beatrice Hall in her work *The Friends of Voltaire*), "I disapprove of what you say, but I will defend to the death your right to say it."[1] According to Ayaan, critical thinking has enriched Christianity more than anything else.

Secondly, Ayaan points out that Islam is especially challenging in 2015 and is worthy of energy and resources: "Islamic extremism threatens the very core of civilization!" It controls the mind and is totalitarian to its core. Islam oppressively mandates that you cannot feel compassion. Ayaan then quotes from the Qur'an: "The woman and the man guilty of adultery or fornication—flog each of them with a hundred stripes: Let not compassion move you in their case, in a matter prescribed by Allah, if ye believe in Allah and the Last Day: and let a party of the Believers witness their punishment" (24.2).

Ayaan then describes a horrific account of a woman in Mogadishu who had complained to a Sharia tribunal about being raped; she is sentenced to death by stoning. An innocent Muslim man a bystander watching her stoning attempts to intervene and is shot on the spot. An eight-year-old boy runs to the aid of the woman and is killed. Islam says you cannot have compassion. The end of civilization as we know it is the inability to show charity and have compassion on others. This is the message of Islam—no compassion on the infidel.

STATUS OF WOMEN IN THE KORAN (12,066 WORDS)

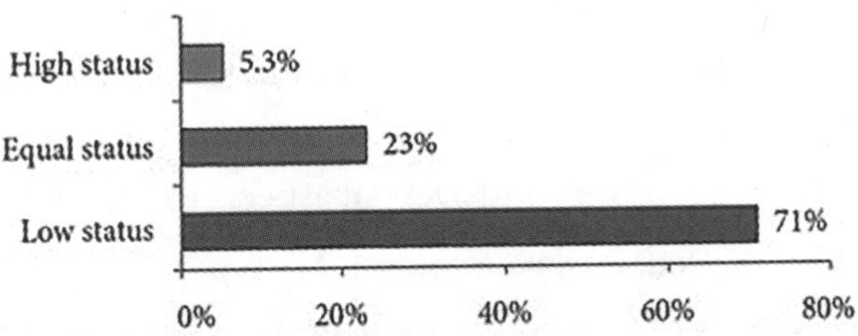

STATISTICS BY VERSE COUNT: WOMEN REFERENCED IN THE QUR'AN		
REFERENCE	**# VERSES**	**% VERSES**
Positive	11	7.3%
Equal	38	25.2%
Negative	102	67.5%
Totals	**151**	

Source: http://www.cspipublishing.com/statistical/TrilogyStats/Womans_Status_in_the_Koran.html.

Finally, Ayaan discusses that not all Muslims are the same, which means that not all Muslims are extremist. There is a growing minority of Muslims who desire reform. Despite the spin job of our government leaders, Ayaan says emphatically that if you want a case study of exactly how Mohammad wanted Islam to be implemented, look at the Islamic State: "If I ever imagined hell, it is the Islamic State." Though too far afield from the purpose of our book, Ayaan, taking a page from Martin Luther's 95 Theses playbook, has proposed five specific reforms to Islam in her latest book *Heretic*. Voices are emerging across the societal spectrum recognizing that radical Islam poses the greatest threat to modern civilization.

Muhammad and the Women

According to Qur'an (33.21) Muhammad "is the Messenger of Allah and an excellent example of character." This may have been the case according to some in the seventh century when Mohammad lived; however, perhaps you should be the judge. While the purpose of this book is not to provide a biography of Mohammad, we have provided some recommended reading in the endnotes on Mohammad's life and will touch on some of the more controversial aspects in this section.

Mohammad endorsed enslavement of all types: he personally owned two "black slaves." "And he bought him for two black slaves, and he did not afterwards take allegiance from anyone until he had asked him whether he was a slave (or a free man)" (Sahih Muslim 10.3901). Muhammad was charitable enough, he endorsed sex-slavery as a gift from Allah, and enjoyed offering sex-slaves as gifts in not one, or two, or three, but in four suras:

> O Prophet! Surely We have made lawful to you your wives whom you have given their dowries, and those whom your right hand possesses out of those whom Allah has given to you as prisoners of war. (Qur'an 33.50)
>
> And if you fear that you cannot act equitably towards orphans, then marry such women as seem good to you, two and three and four; but if you fear that you will not do justice (between them), then (marry) only one or what your right hands possess; this is more proper, that you may not deviate from the right course. (Qur'an 4.3)
>
> And all married women except those whom your right hands possess (this is) Allah's ordinance to you, and lawful for you are (all women) besides those, provided

> that you seek (them) with your property, taking (them) in marriage not committing fornication. Then as to those whom you profit by, give them their dowries as appointed; and there is no blame on you about what you mutually agree after what is appointed; surely Allah is Knowing, Wise. (Qur'an 4.24)
>
> Successful indeed are the believers, Who are humble in their prayers, And who keep aloof from what is vain, And who are givers of poor-rate, And who guard their private parts, Except before their mates or those whom their right hands possess, for they surely are not blameable. (Qur'an 23.1-6)

Bill Warner of the Center for the Study of Political Islam writes:

> Islam has enslaved more people than any other culture. Muslims do not acknowledge this or apologize for their history of enslavement of all races and faiths. A little known fact is that the highest priced slave in Mecca was always a white woman. The Sunna is that Mohammed's favorite sex-slave was a white Christian woman. Islam still practices slavery in Africa. It is found in Saudi Arabia, Mauritania, the Sudan and other Islamic areas that are near Kafirs.[2]

Muhammad enjoyed sex. The Hadith reminds us that Muhammad could have sex with all eleven of his wives in one night:

> Anas bin Malik said, "The Prophet used to visit all his wives in a round, during the day and night and they were eleven in number." I asked Anas, "Had the Prophet the strength for it?" Anas replied, "We used to say that the Prophet was given the strength of thirty (men)." And Sa'id said on the authority of Qatada that Anas had told him about nine wives only (not eleven). (Bukhari 1.5.268)

The Hadith contradicts the Sira's description of Mohammad's sexual strength; relating to Mohammad's endurance, the Qur'an was not all Gabriel gave to Muhammad: "Gabriel met me with a pot, of which I ate and I was given the sexual endurance of forty men" (Tabaqat Ibn Sa'd 8.192). Muhammad had at least eleven wives, but perhaps as many as thirteen. He was in his early fifties when he consummated his marriage to nine-year-old Aisha, his favorite wife: "Unexpectedly Allah's Apostle came to me in the forenoon and my mother handed me over to him, and at that time I was a girl of nine years of age" (Bukhari 5.58.234). Muhammad permitted her to bring her toys and dolls: "'A'isha (Allah be pleased with her) reported that Allah's Apostle (may peace be upon him) married her when she was seven years old, and she was taken to his house as a bride when she was nine, and her dolls were with her; and when he (the Holy Prophet) died she was eighteen years old" (Muslim 8.3311).

Muhammad likened women to a field needing to be harvested in season and out of season: "Your wives are as tilth unto you; so approach your tilth when or how ye will" (Qur'an 2.223). Men who dominate women "are in charge of women," according to the Qur'an, and can be beaten, or as Pickthal translates, "scourged":

> Men are the protectors and maintainers of women, because Allah has given the one more (strength) than the other, and because they support them from their means. Therefore the righteous women are devoutly obedient, and guard in (the husband's) absence what Allah would have them guard. As to those women on whose part ye fear disloyalty and ill-conduct, admonish them (first), (Next), refuse to share their beds, (And last) beat them (lightly). (Qur'an 4.34)

Muhammad sanctioned "temporary marriage" when engaging in Holy War, where the jihadist can temporarily (perhaps for as little as an hour) take on a new wife: "We used to participate in the holy battles led by Allah's Apostle and we had nothing (no wives) with us. So we said, 'Shall we get ourselves castrated?' He forbade us that and then allowed us to marry women with a temporary contract" (Bukhari 7.62.13). The Islamic State is using temporal marriage as a means to rape and brutalize women.

Muhammad said that a man should never be questioned as to why he abused his wife: "The Prophet (peace be upon him) said: A man will not be asked as to why he beat his wife" (Dawud 11.2142). And hell is full of women, predominantly: "The Prophet said: 'I was shown the Hell-fire and that the majority of its dwellers were women who were ungrateful'" (Bukhari 7.62.125). In case the reader missed it, Muhammad revisits women in hell in the next passage: "The Prophet said, 'I looked at Paradise and saw that the majority of its residents were the poor; and I looked at the (Hell) Fire and saw that the majority of its residents were women'" (Bukhari 7.62.126).

Women have no equality and few, if any, rights in Islam. More could be demonstrated. The differences between Islam and Christianity are stark. The apostle Paul commanded husbands to love their wives compassionately and self-sacrificially, writing, "Husbands, love your wives, as Christ loved the church and gave himself up for her" (Ephesians 5:25). The message of the New Testament, recognizing the Judeo-concept of the *Imago Dei* (Genesis 1:27), is equality: "There is neither Jew nor Greek, there is neither slave nor free, there is no male and female, for you are all one in Christ Jesus" (Galatians 3:28).

Jesus said the second greatest commandment after loving God was: "'You shall love your neighbor as yourself.' There is no other commandment greater than these'" (Mark 12:31) With his last words, Jesus ensured that his beloved disciple would look after his mother: "Here is your mother" (John 19.27 NLT). Luke 8 records that women supported Jesus's earthly ministry and those same women were the first witnesses of the resurrected Christ in Luke 24. Women play a central role in Christianity. They are equal, loved, respected, and cherished.

CENTER FOR THE STUDY OF POLITICAL ISLAM

Under Sharia Law:

- There is no freedom of religion.
- There is no freedom of speech.
- There is no freedom of thought.
- There is no freedom of artistic expression.
- There is no freedom of the press.
- There is no equality of peoples—a non-Muslim, a Kafir, is never equal to a Muslim.
- There is no equal protection under Sharia for different classes of people. Justice is dualistic, with one set of laws for Muslim males and different laws for women and non-Muslims.
- There are no equal rights for women.
- Women can be beaten.
- A non-Muslim cannot bear arms.
- There is no democracy, since democracy means that a non-Muslim is equal to a Muslim.
- Our Constitution is a man-made document of ignorance, *jahiliyah,* that must submit to Sharia.
- Non-Muslims are *dhimmis*, third-class citizens.
- All governments must be ruled by Sharia law.
- Unlike common law, Sharia is not interpretive, nor can it be changed.
- There is no golden rule.

CHAPTER 12

CRIMES AGAINST HUMANITY

The Quality of the Tree Is Known by Its Fruit

Perhaps the single biggest factor in prompting many atheists to speak out against belief in God in recent years has been Islamic violence, especially seen in the September 11th attacks against the United States and the surge in terrorist activity since that time. Atheists claim that belief in God leads to divisiveness, hatred, and violence. There is no better evidence for this than the behavior of Muslim extremists and "martyrs" who commit acts of terror and unspeakable atrocities in the name of God. Accordingly, the world would be a better place if humans stopped believing in God.

No doubt reasoning like this accounts for the noticeable upswing toward atheism in the West in recent years. Of course, atheists who argue this way overlook a great deal of evidence that suggests that atheism has been far more harmful to humanity than theism. The brutal history of atheistic Communism, for example, which has been responsible for the deaths of more than 100 million people in the last century or so, is a disturbing case in point. And, of course, atheists who see nothing but evil in theism usually overlook all of the good that has resulted from belief in God.

A Blessing to All Nations

The theism that we have been talking about in this book began with Abraham, a man who lived about 4,000 years ago. It is from him that Judaism, Christianity, and Islam emerged. At the center of the differences between Jews, Christians, and Muslims is how the promises made to the great patriarch are to be interpreted.

We find in the old stories about this famous man what has become known as the "Abrahamic Covenant," an agreement God made with Abraham. It begins with God commanding Abraham to leave Chaldea (in today's Iraq) and migrate westward to the land of Canaan (today's Israel). God promises the patriarch: "I will make of you a great nation, and I will bless you, and make your name great, so that you will be a blessing. I will bless those who bless you, and him who dishonors you I will curse; and in you all the families of the earth shall be blessed" (Genesis 12:2-3 ESV).

This is all well and good, but the problem was that Abraham was childless. When God assures Abraham that his reward will be great, the patriarch asks, "O Lord God, what will you give me, for I continue childless?" God promises Abraham that his descendants will be too numerous to count (Genesis 15:1-6). But Sarah, Abraham's wife, is unable to conceive. Eventually Abraham does have a son, Ishmael, by Sarah's handmaid Hagar (Genesis 16:15). Was the birth of Ishmael the fulfillment of the promise? This is a vital question that needs to be answered.

According to Muslims, the birth of Ishmael, Abraham's first child, is the fulfillment of God's covenant with the great patriarch. But on what basis can Muslims make this claim? Where is their ancient source that supports their interpretation? Our only ancient source is the book of Genesis, whose stories—at least some of them—reach back to the time of Abraham and perhaps even earlier. According to Genesis, Abraham blessed Ishmael, and so did God in response to Abraham's prayer: "As for Ish'mael, I have heard you; behold, I will bless him and make him fruitful and multiply him exceedingly; he shall be the father of twelve princes, and I will make him a great nation" (Genesis 17:20). Ishmael is held in great honor and a great nation of people (the Arabs) did indeed descend from him.

Ishmael was not, however, the fulfillment of God's covenant promise; Isaac was. Abraham himself was more than willing to look upon Ishmael as the fulfillment of the promise (Genesis 17:18). But God spoke otherwise, "No, but Sarah your wife shall bear you a son, and you shall call his name Isaac. I will establish my covenant with him as an everlasting covenant for his descendants after him" (Genesis 17:19). True to this promise, Sarah did conceive in her old age and gave birth to Isaac (Genesis 21:1-7), for whom the covenant was confirmed (Genesis 21:12). It was to Isaac that the aged Abraham "gave all he had" (Genesis 25:5). Together Isaac and Ishmael buried their father (Genesis 25:9).

The covenant with Abraham passed through Isaac to his son Jacob (Genesis 27:30; 28:21), who became the father of twelve sons (Genesis 35:22), and whose name was later changed to Israel (Genesis 32:28). It is from these sons that the twelve tribes of Israel sprang. They became known as the Hebrew people, though they called themselves Israelites and their home country, which at one time was the land of the Philistines (from which we derive the later name Palestine), was known as Israel. This land was settled sometime between 1500 and 1300 BC. Israel's first kings—Saul, David, and Solomon—reigned in the 900s BC. Their stories and those of their royal successors are told in the Old Testament's books of Samuel and Kings.

Jews and Christians alike accept the narrative that we have just recounted. How much of it is literal history is debated, of course. But much of it is accepted by many because the narratives are ancient and reflect the times and customs of the peoples who are part of the story. It is not accepted in the Qur'an and Islamic traditions, however. In fact, the key element of the story is turned on its head: Isaac does not receive the blessing; Ishmael does. How did Muhammad know this? Was there another ancient source, more reliable historically, perhaps better supported by archaeology? No. Muhammad knows this because God told him (through the angel Gabriel).

The problem with this approach is that one can always claim God as proof for whatever one claims. Corroborating evidence is not needed. God revealed it and that settles it. But what if God really didn't reveal it? How would anyone know? That is where evidence plays an essential role. Historians will not trust an ancient document unless there is evidence that suggests that the document is in fact credible. This is why archaeology and topography are so important for the study of the Bible. Historians, archaeologists, and biblical scholars trust the narratives (with the usual disagreements among them about this and that detail) because the narratives and the physical evidence correlate. The narratives exhibit verisimilitude, as has already been said.

Archaeology and other historical sources show that the Holy Land in the time of the patriarchs really was the way it is reflected in the book of Genesis. The Ancient Near Eastern tablets and inscriptions correlate with most of the stories in the early chapters of Genesis. The Ebla Tablets found in Syria, as well as other sources, show that names like Abraham are authentic to the time in which Abraham and his immediate descendants lived. Archaeology in Egypt shows that Israel's references to building a certain way while the Hebrews lived in Egypt are authentic. Archaeological excavations in Israel today attest the existence of the ancient kingdom of Israel in the days of Saul, David, and Solomon. The results of these excavations show that Jerusalem really was the capital city of a small empire extending to the southern boundaries of Lebanon in the north and the desert regions of Edom, Moab, and Sinai in the south.

Nothing like this can be said with regard to the Qur'an. There is no archaeological evidence that supports Muhammad's radical recasting of the ancient biblical narrative. He has rewritten parts of it so that his understanding of God and the Arab people receive support from Israel's history and principal characters in that history. In essence, the Qur'an, which devout Muslims follow uncritically and without question, represents a massive revision of history that utterly lacks corroboration from archaeology or other historical sources.

As a result of this rewriting of Israel's ancient history, Muslims today completely reject Israel's claim to its homeland. As a modern nation, Israel itself is not only not recognized, but the entire history of Israel has been hijacked and turned into an Islamic history. The utter anachronism of this approach goes unnoticed by almost all Muslims (indeed, by many non-Muslims). Not surprisingly, Muslims believe that the Jewish people have no right to live in the Holy Land. They think the state of Israel has no legitimacy. Some Muslim countries do not even show Israel on maps of the Middle East. Zealous Muslims will never make peace with Israel but will continue to do everything possible to destroy this small country and drive out or kill the Jewish people.

Criminal Intent

This is the theological backdrop to the radical ideology we see at work in the Middle East and in other parts of the world today. Many westerners naively believe that Muslims strongly oppose Israel because the Palestinians have been treated (in their view) unjustly. The violence practiced by radical Muslim groups against the Palestinians, especially the Christian Palestinians, is hardly noticed. As Israel has learned the hard way, left to themselves the West Bank and Gaza Strip have become occupied by terrorist groups who have no interest in the well-being of the Palestinians and certainly no desire to form lasting peace with Israel.

Radical Islam desires to capture the world for Islam and will use any means necessary to achieve this goal. Iran desires to obtain nuclear weapons so that it might intimidate the West and, if possible, destroy Israel. If such actions result in the destruction of Iran, then so be it: it is the will of Allah. ISIS is attempting to form a new caliphate in the Middle East, whereby it can consolidate its gains and project its power throughout the world, that it might further its mission of radical Islamic conquest. Most, of course, agree that ISIS is violent and its tactics are abhorrent, but does it truly represent Islam?

United States President Barack Obama doesn't think so. He has on more than one occasion said to the effect that ISIS "is not 'Islamic.' No religion condones the killing of innocents, and the vast majority of [ISIS]'s victims have been Muslim."[1] Many have reacted to these assertions with skepticism. Indeed, honest and thoughtful Muslims do not agree with the president. Two weeks after Obama's speech, British Muslim Maajid Nawaz remarked on Facebook:

> We Muslims must admit there are challenging Koranic passages that require reinterpretation today. Let us use existing tools of exegesis, such as specificity, restriction, abrogation and metaphor. Vacuous literalism as an interpretive method must be abandoned. It is bankrupt. Only by rejecting vacuous literalism are we able to condemn, in principle, ISIS-style slavery, beheading, lashing, amputation and other medieval practices forever (all of which are in the Qur'an). This is a struggle within Islam.[2]

Everyone should be encouraged by Nawaz's sensible recommendation. When he speaks of the use of "tools of exegesis," he is describing what Jews and Christians do when they interpret the Bible. There are violent texts in the Bible, in narratives that describe the history of Israel and in oracles and poetry that speak metaphorically and hyperbolically. Jewish and Christian interpreters do not apply these texts in a wooden and literalistic fashion without regard to the ancient context and original circumstances that today no longer apply. Would that more Muslims and Islamic clerics and teachers appreciated what Nawaz has said.

But it will not be easy, perhaps not even possible, for most Muslims to move away from traditional understandings of Islam and the teaching of the Qur'an. The reason for this is that the Qur'an itself forbids freethinking and raising honest questions:

> But no, by your Lord, they can have no faith, until they make you (Muhammad) judge in all disputes between them, and find in themselves no resistance against your decisions, and accept (them) with full submission. (Qur'an 4.65)
>
> It is not for a believer, man or woman, when Allah and His Messenger have decreed a matter, that they should have any option in their decision. And whoever disobeys Allah and His Messenger, he has indeed strayed in a plain error. (Qur'an 33.36)

This teaching places a devout Muslim in a very difficult position. No matter how arcane a teaching might be, no matter how dubious, no matter how violent, it is not to be questioned. This becomes a huge problem when one considers how many hateful statements are present in the Qur'an. We shall consider a few examples.

"We said to them (Jews): 'Be apes, despised and hated'" (2.65; see also 5.59-60: Allah "made of them apes and pigs, and worshippers of idols"; 7.166). In Maulana Muhammad Ali's commentary on the Qur'an, he explains that this verse teaches that the Jewish people were not turned into apes with respect to their outer appearance, but with respect to the transformation of their hearts. Ali even appeals to the Jewish Bible (Ezekiel 22:8-15) as offering additional support for the Qur'an's outrageous assertion.[3] Nowhere does Ali express any embarrassment for the Qur'an's egregious racism.

Jews are cursed or criticized in many passages. Here is just one more example:

> The Jews have said, "Allah's hand is tied up." Their hands are shackled, and they are cursed for what they have said. No, but His hands are outspread. He disperses as He pleases. And what has been sent down to you from your Lord will surely increase many of them in insolence and unbelief.... They hasten about the earth, to do corruption there. And Allah loves not the workers of corruption. (Qur'an 5.64)

Ali explains that the Jews practiced usury and made themselves rich. Therefore they taunted poor Muslims by suggesting that Allah's hand was "tied up" or fettered and so could not help them. On the contrary, because Allah's hands are "outspread," Muslims (but not Jews or Christians) may anticipate material and spiritual benefits.[4]

Believers will be terrorized:

> When your Lord revealed to the angels: "I am with you; so confirm the believers. I shall cast into the unbelievers' hearts terror; so smite above the necks, and smite every finger of them!" (Qur'an 8.12)

Violent statements such as this are common in the Qur'an. The devout Muslim is to fight infidels until the religion of Allah prevails (8.39). The Muslim is to know that Allah will repay the Muslim fighter whatever he expends in fighting unbelievers (8.60). Allah commands Muhammad to "strive (jihad) hard against the unbelievers," for their end will be hell (9.73; 98.6). The devout Muslim is to "fight those who do not believe in Allah...and do not forbid what Allah and His Messenger have forbidden" (9.29). Muslims are to "slay the idolaters wherever you find them, and take them, and confine them, and lie in wait for them at every place of ambush" (9.5). "When you meet the unbelievers, smite their necks" (47.4).

The last three statements very much reflect the violence we see today. Muslim extremists, especially the Taliban that once dominated Afghanistan, and now the Islamic State, which controls parts of Iraq and Syria, are forcing their understanding of Sharia law on those they conquer. And of course, as westerners have come to learn well since September 11th, Islamic terrorists take hostages and confine them and lie in wait to ambush anyone they regard as enemies. Even more recently, the civilized world has recoiled in horror at the public video recordings of the beheadings of hostages.

Civilized people regard the activities of these Muslim extremists as criminal and morally indefensible. It is no wonder that generous-minded people, including Islam's apologists, claim that these terrible actions do not really represent Islam. But alas, they do. In many places the Qur'an teaches violence against "unbelievers," including Jews and Christians. Mercy is shown only when people submit to Islam (and remember, Islam means "submission"). The actions of the Islamic State, in which this organization wishes to reestablish a caliphate after the model of Abu Bakr, the first caliph, represents the original vision and mission of the founders of Islam. It is not a coincidence that the current leader of the Islamic State calls himself Abu Bakr al-Baghdadi, or "Abu Bakr of Baghdad."[5]

Paradise Gained or Paradise Lost?

We have all heard how the young Muslim men today who are persuaded to go into battle against the infidels are promised seventy-two virgins in paradise. Allah's followers "kill and are killed" (Qur'an 9.111), but they will receive paradise. They should "rejoice in the bargain (they) have made with" Allah. In other words, paradise is worth dying for.

Devout Muslims are promised a lot of things, but the promise of seventy-two virgins is quite doubtful. In a Hadith it is stated that Muhammad was heard to say that Muslims in paradise will enjoy the benefits of thousands of servants and, especially, seventy-two *houris*, that is, pure, beautiful maidens (*Jami' at-Tirmidhi* 2687). However, it is not at all clear that the Qur'an or Muhammad ever spoke of "seventy-two." It has been suggested that the tradition of "seventy-two virgins" is based on references to "seventy-two grapes (or raisins)" or "seventy-two angels." Nevertheless, the Qur'an definitely promises carnal rewards.

Whatever we think about the tradition of the "seventy-two virgins,"[6] all devout Muslims—both men and women—are promised "companions," or *houris*. It is assumed, therefore, that the *houris* will exist in both genders. In Qur'an 52.20 God "will join them (i.e., faithful Muslims) to pure, beautiful ones." The verses that follow promise food and drink (52.22-23). The faithful may be assured that "around them go boys of theirs as if they were hidden pearls" (52.24). Similarly it is promised in 56.17, "Round about them will go youths never growing old," which are "pure, beautiful ones, likened to hidden pearls; a reward for what they did" (56.22-24). Even the spouses of Muslims will be recreated in paradise as *houris* (40.8; 56.34-36). Muslim men no doubt are delighted to learn that the *houris* who will be given to them are not only youthful but will have large breasts (78.33).[7]

In the Hadith and Medieval commentators, these Qur'anic traditions are interpreted and expanded. For example, Muslims are assured that no one will be in paradise without a wife (*Sahih Muslim* 6793). Muhammad al-Bukhari explains that each man in paradise will have two wives from among the *houris*, who will be beautiful, pure, and in some sense transparent (*Sahih al-Bukhari* 54.476). Al-Bukhari goes on to say that these *houris* do not urinate, defecate, or have runny noses (55.544). Old women who enter paradise will be made into young, beautiful virgins; all will be perfect, and so forth.

All of this will strike most westerners as incredibly naïve, even bizarre (not to mention lustful), but for the men of the Middle East in the Medieval period it was a way of imagining a wonderful life, beyond the barrenness and limited opportunities with which so many of them lived. It was also a powerful, motivating force to join the swelling ranks of the armies of Islam and risk life and limb in battle. If the battle is won and one survives, then there is booty and captured women. If one dies in battle, there will be food, drink, and beautiful companions in paradise. Either way, one can't lose.

Not only are promises of paradise and sexual fantasies motivating factors in the current ISIS-driven war in the Middle East, so is an interesting doctrine of eschatology, or "last things." We refer to the belief in the soon coming of an anointed figure, called the Mahdi (lit. "Guided One"), thought to be a descendant from the family of Muhammad. His coming will coincide with the second coming of Jesus Christ. Indeed, the returning Christ will assist the Mahdi in defeating the *Masih ad-Dajjal*, or "false messiah" (or anti-Christ). The Mahdi will destroy unbelievers and finish the work of converting the world to Islam. The Mahdi's warriors will carry black flags (which is why ISIS has adopted the black flag), and Israel will finally be conquered and surviving Jews and Christians will recognize that Muhammad really was God's greatest prophet and that Islam is the true religion. The wicked (called Gog and Magog) will gather for one last battle, and Allah will defeat them and then all of humanity will appear before him for judgment.

This Islamic eschatology (which differs at points among Sunnis and Shias) does not derive from Muhammad or the Qur'an but seems to have begun its development a half century or so after Muhammad's death. It draws heavily and creatively on the Bible and various Jewish and Christian traditions (e.g., the return of Jesus Christ, the final defeat of the wicked, the day of judgment). Like many other Islamic teachings, it is another example of hijacking Jewish and Christian traditions and taking them in new directions. It is quite remarkable that Jesus has been transformed into the Mahdi's assistant.

The Islamic quest for paradise, paradoxically, is leading to murder, mayhem, and chaos. Fortunately, moderate Muslims do not support ISIS and other terrorist organizations. But very few moderate Muslims speak out against these groups. We believe this is the case because in part Muslims actually agree with most of the theology that lies behind the ideology. It is, after all, rooted in the Qur'an and early Islamic traditions, such as the Hadith. ISIS and other extremists know this and so regard moderate Muslims as having a weak, compromised faith if they do not actively support today's militant jihad against Israel, the West, and all unbelievers and apostates who get in the way.

The bad news for the world is that radical Islam will not go away anytime soon. Thanks to modern communication, computers, the Internet, and social media, terrorist organizations will continue to recruit, train, and arm fanatics who are "willing to kill and be killed." The good news is that despite persecution, the peace-making gospel of Jesus is spreading among Muslims in the Middle East. We can only hope that the Christian faith, which originated in the Holy Land, will make a strong comeback. The only hope for a lasting peace in the Middle East is Jesus and his way, not the coercive, threatening violence of Islam.

CONCLUSION

TO DEFEND AGAINST MUHAMMAD'S FAITH, EVEN IF YOU ARE UNABLE TO DEFEND YOURSELF AGAINST HIS SWORD

Martin Luther's Lessons on Responding to Islam

Nearly a half-millennium ago, Martin Luther (1483–1586), along with continental Europe, faced the horrors of the Ottoman caliphate, led by the bloodthirsty Suleiman the Magnificent. For nearly fifty years Suleiman led the Turks into its golden age, expanding the caliphate and with it threatening the whole of Europe. In 1529, only four hundred miles from Luther's front door, an estimated 120,000 Turks, led by Suleiman, stormed the city of Vienna. Amazingly, the Viennese protectors, numbering less than 20,000, with help from a hostile European early winter, were able to hold off the behemoth Turkish advance. Luther perceived the Ottoman expansion as not only a geo-political threat to Europe, but an aggressive challenge to Christianity.

Figure 1 – Luther's Qur'an (c. 1543). Photo courtesy of J. J. Johnston

As my wife and I made the ninety-minute journey from Berlin to Wittenberg, officially Lutherstadt (Luther City) Wittenberg, we were not aware of Luther's interest in and publishing prowess on Islam. Little did we know that the most memorable experience of our visit to Lutherstadt would not be seeing the 95 Theses incised on the bronze doors of the north portal of the Schloßkirche (All Saint's Church), nor would it be Luther House where while studying Romans he experienced his personal awakening that led to the Reformation, nor would it be gazing in the Luther Room at the famed "Table" where Luther's students and colleagues joined him for meals and excited yet terse theological conversations we now call *Table Talks*. Rather, what astounded me was when I noticed an ancient book with a Latin title "ALCORANVS," or Qur'an. The story behind Luther's Qur'an is both fascinating and little known. Luther's example of a Christian response to sixteenth-century Islamic aggression is exemplary and relevant to our modern-day response to the rise of the Islamic State.

Martin Luther, like many Christians today, never met or interacted with a Muslim; however, unlike most modern Christians, that did not stop him from educating himself and others about the threat of Islam. In his lessons on Joel 2, Luther refers to the domination and success of the Turks[1] as the "scourge of God":

> Almost everywhere they (Turks) come out as successful victors while our armies succumb. They certainly will finally overcome us, for they are very evidently the scourge of God. Therefore, just as we are accustomed to preach about the coming of the Turks, the prophet did the same thing in this chapter.[2]

Indeed, in his preface on Ezekiel, Luther saw the Turkish invasion as the dawning of the last days, as he interpreted the Ottoman caliphate as the Gog foretold in Ezekiel 38–39:

> SINCE the Revelation of St. John, chapter 20[:8-9], describes how Gog with his great army, as innumerable as the sand by the sea, battles against Christendom, and how in the end he will be destroyed by fire from heaven—and we consider this ["Gog"] to be the Turk—I have undertaken while I am sitting here so idly to translate into German also the two chapters of Ezekiel, the thirty-eighth and thirty-ninth, which correspond in almost every point with the Revelation.[3]

Luther recognized the caliphate was a legitimate threat. His response was information and education. In his 1530 preface to the *Book on the Ceremonies of the Turks,* Luther stated that since the Turks were lurking in their own backyards and knocking at their doors, the Christians must be "warned" and they must "learn" the religion of Muhammad in order to counteract it.[4] It took twelve years for Luther to finally receive a Latin copy of the Qur'an so he could verify if all the horrors and tragedies he had heard and read of Islam were actually authorized by Muhammad. Finally on February 21, 1542 (thirteen years after writing his first treatise on Islam *Against the Turks*), Luther obtained a Latin manuscript of the Qur'an and was finally able to study from the fount of Islam. And to his utter amazement nothing he had previously learned about Islamic treatment of women or the infidel was overstated.

An improved Latin translation of the Qur'an was urgently needed in the sixteenth century. However, printing the Qur'an in Europe at this time was a criminal offense, as Johannes Oporinus, a publisher from Basil, Switzerland, personally experienced. On December 2, 1542, Martin Luther wrote a letter to the council at Basil urging Oporinus's release. Luther not only supported the publication of the Qur'an, but he included a polemical preface to be included in its publication. The council agreed and released Oporinus to finish the project. In 1543 "Luther's Qur'an" was published using Thomas Bibliander's critical translation, parts of the Hadith, and included other prefaces reacting to Islamic faith and practice.

Luther's preface to the Qur'an in 1543 reveals his passion that followers of Jesus not be ignorant of the teaching of Muhammad, thereby equipping them to have an answer to the false claims of Islam based on historical, evidential, and theological bedrock. In fact, Luther went so far as to say the church was suffering because of her ignorance. Luther's preface was driven by apologetic goals to equip and arm the church to "read the writings of their enemies—so that they may more accurately refute, strike, and overturn those writings, so that they may be able to correct some of them, or at least to fortify our own people with stronger arguments."[5]

After careful analysis of the Qur'an, Luther wrote a preface to *Refutation of the Qur'an,* which was originally published in the early fourteenth century by Ricoldo da Monte di Croce and therein offered his own repudiation, "so that we Germans, too, may know what a shameful faith the faith of Mohammed is, and in order to strengthen us in our Christian faith."[6] Luther enumerated several contradictions within the Qur'an itself. Never one to mince words and far from a distorted view of the prophet, following his careful study Luther remarked, "Mohammed has tormented Christians more horribly than all tyrants."[7]

Luther saw inconsistencies with Muslims, especially in their mistreatment of women:

> For anyone who, in accordance with Mohammed's law, takes as many wives as he wants, divorces them again, and takes them back again as often as he wishes, or sells them, etc., is no husband but a genuine pimp or a whoremonger. God has not so created women nor has He appointed them to be treated like this, as, in addition to reason itself, Moses and the Gospel also teach us.[8]

Particularly inspirational is Martin Luther's reason for writing such a refutation to the Qur'an: so that all "will be able to defend themselves against the faith of Mohammed, even if they were unable to defend themselves against his sword."[9]

Back to Lutherstadt, as we stood in Luther House and gazed at the 1543 Qur'an sanctioned by Martin Luther, we were inspired, even encouraged, by Luther's leadership and example. These are very challenging times for Christians all over the world. Islamic aggression is a threat not only to Christendom, but also against Western civilization itself. We need a thinking church. We are concerned about Christian witness and testimony coming across unthinkingly ignorant of Islam. We need to emulate the leaders from Issachar in First Chronicles 12:32: "From Issachar there were 200 leaders and all their relatives at their command—they understood the times and knew what Israel should do" (NET). Do we understand the times we are living in so that we can arrive at a solution? In an age of racial skepticism and

Islamic aggression, Luther still speaks to us today. The church cannot be caught off-guard and unprepared. We must follow Luther's example and understand Islam more clearly to be more effective in introducing Muslims to the grace of our Lord Jesus Christ and the assurance and hope that can only be found in Him.

Finally, we are delighted by numerous reports of Muslims coming to faith in the authentic, biblical Jesus from all around the world. In the past decade an ever-increasing number of Muslims have reported seeing Jesus in visions and dreams and coming to faith in him for redemption and forgiveness.

The writer of Hebrews writes: "Long ago, at many times and in many ways, God spoke to our fathers by the prophets, but in these last days he has spoken to us by his Son, whom he appointed the heir of all things, through whom also he created the world" (Hebrews 1:1-2 ESV). Our hope is that you might enter into a relationship with Jesus Christ, the Prince of Peace. If you follow Jesus, our challenge is for you to embody a restorative, thinking faith, evidencing love and compassion for Muslims throughout the world. "By this all people will know that you are my disciples, if you have love for one another" (John 13:35 ESV).

SPECIAL REPORT

THE ISLAMIC STATE AS A MILITARY ACTOR

by Harry R. Gorham

The Islamic State (IS) should not be thought of as a terrorist group in the classical sense, but as a qualitative progression of the model developed by al-Qaeda and other non-state actors. Under the leadership of Abu Bakr al-Baghdadi, the Islamic State has metastasized into a state entity with a formidable military force. Through a well-coordinated and executed military campaign, the Islamic State now controls large areas of both Syria and Iraq. From an operational point of view, the IS has demonstrated that it is capable of conducting and coordinating sophisticated military operations within a relatively large geographical area. Not only is it a professional military force, but it also functions as a practical model for governance, which has proven to be surprisingly resilient and effective within an unstable environment.[1]

As a military force, the Islamic State is comparable to other contemporary insurgent groups, such as the Taliban, Hezbollah, or Hamas. In addition to its political and religious components, the Islamic State retains a conventional military force that is well trained, motivated, and equipped with advanced weaponry and munitions. Its success on the battlefield is attributable to its ability to adopt a range of different styles of warfare. This hybridized approach to warfare includes terrorism, guerrilla-style operations, and conventional maneuvers. Its operations also display a rapid evolution of tactics, such as suicide bombing, and innovation in weaponry and armaments, which include the use of suicide vehicle-borne improvised explosive devices (SVBIEDs).[2]

The Islamic State has also demonstrated an ability to operate in a complex and fluid environment. To coincide with a professionally executed and designed military strategy, the IS has implemented a methodical and deliberate attempt to incite sectarian violence, exploit political impotence, and exert brutal violence to control a population. In conjunction with their success on the battlefield, the Islamic State has also developed a near-complete mode of governance, which, when combined with the organization's ability to generate revenue, has been able to exert effective control over the territory that it currently occupies.

Unlike other Islamic militant or insurgent groups, the IS is unique as it seeks to hold territory and govern. It has therefore established a conventional style military organization that resembles a modern army. This study will examine the evolution of the Islamic State as a military hybrid force and its strategy to expand and defend the caliphate. Through this evaluation, the Islamic State will be presented as an adaptive military actor that has proven to be resourceful and innovative. In order to effectively counter the IS as a regional threat, a thorough understanding of its force structure and military strategy must be understood.

The Evolution of the Islamic State as a Military Actor

The Islamic State as a military force evolved through progressive stages. The first stage, which occurred between 2003 and 2011, can be characterized as a deliberate terrorism campaign that was directed primarily against the Shia population and US forces operating in Iraq. During this phase, the IS employed an indiscriminate campaign of violence and terror which sought to stoke the sectarian animosity between the Sunni and Shia communities in Iraq.

The second stage can be characterized as a guerrilla insurgency that expanded into Syria and northern Iraq toward the beginning of 2011. The Syrian civil war, in conjunction with the growing Sunni discontent toward the Shia-dominated government in Baghdad, created the conditions for the Islamic State to expand and project its extremist brand of Islam. It was during this period that the IS transitioned from a terrorist organization into a mobile conventional army and implemented a well-coordinated campaign to conquer terrain in both Iraq and Syria.

The third stage emanates from a theological and political necessity to consolidate gains within the territories it seized since the establishment of the caliphate in June 2014. In order to institute the political and social structures needed to establish the caliphate as a legitimate state entity, the Islamic State will attempt to consolidate the terrain it currently controls. In order for the IS to exert control in these territories and expand the Islamic caliphate, it will attempt to dissolve the states of Iraq and Syria through a protracted campaign of hybrid warfare.

Although it can trace its origins as far back as 1999 in Afghanistan, the Islamic State can be directly linked to a Sunni Islamist group that was established by Abu Musab al-Zarqawi in Iraq in October 2004. Initially known as Tanzim Qaeda al-Jihad fi Bilad al-Rafidayn, or al-Qaeda in Iraq (AQI), Zarqawi pledged fealty, or *bay'a*, to the authority of Osama bin Laden. Zarqawi would subsequently develop a series of Sunni insurgent groups to expand upon al-Qaeda's presence and influence and exploit regional instability. The most capable of these groups was the Islamic State in Iraq (ISI), which would eventually transition into the Islamic State in Iraq and the Levant (ISIL) in 2013.

Under the leadership of Abu Musab al-Zarqawi, AQI operated as a Salafist jihadist group that utilized terrorism to ignite sectarian violence in Iraq. Motivated by an extremist view of Islam, Zarqawi orchestrated a protracted terror campaign that attempted to initiate a civil war in Iraq. From 2003 to 2007, AQI targeted the Shia community and their holy sites, including the Imam al-Askari shrine in 2006, in an effort to provoke them to retaliate against Sunnis. Although at the time the US was the occupying power in Iraq, Zarqawi viewed the Shia as a greater threat. He believed that the US forces would eventually withdraw from Iraq, leaving the Shia in control of the government. According to Zarqawi, a sectarian war would ultimately result in a Sunni victory.

However, AQI became increasingly violent and notorious for its use of indiscriminate, mass-casualty attacks that frequently included suicide bombings. The targeting of civilian and religious targets alienated AQI from the Sunni population. The leadership of al-Qaeda began to question the ideology and strategy that Zarqawi employed. Ayman al-Zawahiri, al-Qaeda's second-in-command at the time, criticized Zarqawi for his indiscriminate use of violence and attempts to ignite a sectarian conflict between Shia and Sunni in Iraq. Zawahiri contended that Shia Muslims were not necessarily infidels who could be fought, but should be excused on account that their theological errors were linked to ignorance.[3] Nonetheless, both Zarqawi and the leadership of al-Qaeda believed that an Islamic emirate, or caliphate, should be carved out of Iraq once US forces had withdrawn. It was at this stage that AQI began to expand upon its military capabilities in order to establish an embryonic caliphate in Iraq.

AQI reached the pinnacle of its destructive capacity toward the end of 2006. The efforts made by US and coalition forces, combined with the support of the Arab Awakening (Sahwa) Council in 2006, flushed AQI out of its protective enclaves. As part of a "surge" strategy, these operations severely degraded most of AQI's operational capabilities.[4] On June 7, 2006, Zarqawi was killed in a US airstrike. Subsequent operations by US ground and air forces pounded AQI further, and succeeded in removing them from safe havens in and around Baghdad, as well as within other Sunni communities such as Mosul, Fallujah, Diyala, and Salah ad-Din.[5] These operations continued throughout 2006 and 2007, and succeeded in reducing the organization to such a degree that only a fraction of its operational capabilities remained.

However, al-Qaeda and the remaining leadership of AQI proved to be resilient, as they continued to coordinate high-profile suicide and mass casualty attacks across Iraq. Zawahiri urged jihadists in Iraq to continue on with their efforts to establish a caliphate in Iraq. While a relationship between al-Qaeda in Pakistan and Afghanistan and AQI was established, the latter never became fully subordinate to al-Qaeda. In many ways, the leadership of al-Qaeda demonstrated minimal interest toward the establishment of a caliphate that it had previously advocated for. According to Cole Brunzel and other Middle Eastern scholars, this lack of enthusiasm was largely attributable to the fact that al-Qaeda had lost control of the state-building process and grown weary of the extremist ideology that was espoused by the leadership of AQI.[6]

On October 12, 2006, the leadership of AQI formed an alliance with several jihadi militant groups and Sunni tribal leaders in Iraq. This affiliation was initially referred to as "Alliance of the Scented Ones," which would later be renamed the "Islamic State of Iraq." The purpose of the Islamic State of Iraq (ISI) was to carve out a territory in Iraq and establish a state for the Sunni population. The ISI's newly proclaimed media spokesman, Muharib al-Jubar, identified the new leader of ISI as Abu Bakr al-Baghdadi, or the "Commander of the Faithful."[7]

By the end of 2010, AQI began to once again capitalize on Sunni disenfranchisement in Iraq. Under the government of Nouri al-Maliki, the Sunni minority were politically sidelined and prosecuted. In an effort to foment sectarianism, AQI launched a protracted terror campaign that included a series of sophisticated suicide bombing operations that targeted government infrastructure and Shia holy sites. While these efforts failed to provoke Shia violence directly, they demonstrated that AQI's operational capabilities were evolving. Fatalities in Iraq rose above five hundred during the initial months of 2012. These operations involved multiple suicide attacks and were directed primarily against Shia targets in cities such as Basra, Karbala, and Nasiriya. AQI also began to step up its efforts against the Iraqi government in February as they initiated a series of well-coordinated attacks against the police and Iraqi Security Forces (ISF). On March 4, 2012, AQI conducted a large-scale raid on ISF units stationed in Anbar province, near the city of Haditha. During this operation they assassinated two police chiefs and occupied a military checkpoint, killing twenty-seven ISF and police personnel.[8]

In June 2012 AQI took a key step in its evolution and development. Capitalizing on the momentum it had gained in March, AQI initiated the "Breaking the Walls" campaign. In a speech delivered on the Internet, al-Baghdadi indicated that the purpose of this operation was to regain territory in Iraq and secure the release of prisoners. Over the course of this twelve-month operation, AQI conducted twenty simultaneous vehicle-borne improvised explosive device (VBIEDs) attacks, eight major raids on prison instillations, and a consolidation of territory.[9] In an effort to incite sectarian violence, AQI shifted its focus toward the Shia community in Baghdad. This phase represented the last component of the "Breaking the Walls" campaign. It also coincided with a broad mobilization of sectarian affiliates across Iraq as Shia militias and al-Qaeda affiliates became increasingly involved in the Syrian civil war. However, AQI achieved all of its operational objectives as it generated more manpower through the prison breaks and killed close to one hundred and twenty ISF and police personnel.[10]

The recruitment of former Baathist army and intelligence officers from Saddam's military also had a significant impact on AQI and its ability to coordinate and plan large-scale operations. According to Jessica Lewis McFate, AQI likely benefitted from the expertise of veterans who had fought against US forces during the occupation and with the Syrian opposition fighting against the Assad regime.[11] It was during this period that AQI began to reorganize their command and control network, logistical support elements, and field units in an effort to increase their presence in northern Iraq and Syria.

As the Syrian conflict escalated and radicalized, AQI devoted significant resources toward the capture of Syrian territory. Control of territory in Iraq remained one of AQI's most important political and military objectives, but under al-Baghdadi, governing Syria was also of significant importance. In a symbolic move, al-Baghdadi changed the name of AQI to the Islamic State in Iraq and the Levant (ISIL). He also claimed that the largest of the Syrian Islamist groups, Jabhat al-Nusra, would now fall under the operational control of ISIL.[12] The leadership of al-Qaeda responded to this edict by issuing a statement that challenged the authority of al-Baghdadi.

The emir of Jabhat al-Nusra, Abu Muhammad al-Jawlani, refused to be integrated into ISIL's command network and pledged his support to the leader of al-Qaeda, Ayman al-Zawahiri. The ideological differences between al-Qaeda and al-Baghdadi became increasingly evident during this period as well. In various statements, Zawahiri openly questioned the strategy and rationale of establishing an Islamic caliphate in both Syria and Iraq. From a strategic and operational point of view, al-Baghdadi and the military leadership of ISIL viewed Iraq and Syria as one theater of operations that should function under a single command network. They expected that the ability to operate in both Syria and Iraq would enable ISIL to move their forces freely along the border and take advantage of this vast space to consolidate gains, control populated centers, and operate in depth.

Despite the objections of Zawahiri, ISIL moved into Syria and recruited thousands of jihadi fighters into its ranks. This move was not tolerated by Jabhat al-Nusra, nor by any of the moderate insurgent groups operating in Syria. In May, Zawahiri intervened and released a directive that annulled ISIL's encroachment into Syria and ordered the two factions to remain separate organizations that were to operate in Syria and Iraq respectively.[13] However, al-Baghdadi refused to recognize the authority of Zawahiri and, as the "Commander of the Faithful," he began to shift ISIL ground forces and military assets to the Syrian front, which was beginning to center around Raqqa.

In Syria, ISIL initiated various public relations campaigns in an effort to foster popular support amongst the Sunni population. An elaborate attempt was made to pacify the Sunni population and absorb them under localized control. Nevertheless, their brutality and extremist behavior prompted other Sunni and Islamist groups to halt the advances made by ISIL. Although the emergence of an anti-ISIL front in Syria in early 2014 resulted in the loss of territory and personnel, these setbacks were temporary and only slight. During this period, mounting Sunni grievances with al-Maliki's government provided ISIL with an opportunity to establish effective control in northern Iraq. In Allepo province, ISIL was able to deploy large mobile infantry groups, which served as reinforcements for ISIL units operating in Syria. This additional manpower allowed ISIL to attack Jabhat al-Nusra positions around the city of Raqqa, which had been captured from the Syrian army in March 2013. On January 14, ISIL forces moved into Raqqa and secured the city.

The fall of Raqqa provided ISIL with a staging point to expand its military operations in both Syria and Iraq. It also became a prototype for Islamic governance, as it demonstrated the forms of control that

ISIL intended to implement within the territories that it occupied.[14] After seizing and consolidating around the newly established capitol, ISIL forces seized and occupied Fallujah and Ramadi, two largely Sunni cities, in January 2014. This operation marked a shift toward a more conventional approach in the military strategy of ISIL, as it now focused on establishing overt territorial control in northern Iraq in order to develop staging points for its operations in Anbar province and other areas along the Syrian border.[15]

ISIL now focused its operations along the Khabur and Euphrates rivers, as it initiated coordinated attacks against opposition groups in eastern Syria. These attacks opened the border between Syria and Iraq, allowing for ISIL to move freely between two different fronts. As a result, weapons, fighters, and money crossed the border more frequently.[16] On June 6, ISIL fighters commenced an offensive to seize Mosul, the second largest city in Iraq. It took only four days for it to fall. In many ways, the capture of Mosul was a complete and astonishing victory. The ISIL force that seized Mosul was composed of 1,300 fighters against the ISF, which numbered around 60,000. The numbers, however, do not serve to highlight the operational effectiveness of ISIL, as they are an indication of the incompetence and corruption of the ISF. According to certain estimates, only about one in three Iraqi soldiers was present in Mosul during the time of the assault, the remainder were paying their salaries to ISF officers in order to remain at home or stay on permanent leave.[17]

The capture of Mosul was a well-executed operation in urban warfare. It incorporated guerrilla tactics into combined arms operations and demonstrated an ability to coordinate and maneuver large troop formations in combat. The assault began with five suicide bombings that were supported by mortar fire. Other Sunni insurgent groups joined ISIL units as well, including the Baathist Naqshbandi and the Ansar al-Islam. During the attack, ISIL units utilized pickup trucks to infiltrate the city, overrunning ISF checkpoints and other security instillations with little difficulty.

On the second day of the assault, ISIL fighters had maneuvered from the south to attack the city in key areas. They combined conventional style urban operations with suicide vehicle-borne improvised explosive devices (SVBIEDs) to great effect, striking police and military targets simultaneously. The ISF used helicopters to target ISIL forces, but they proved difficult to identify in an urban setting. After these attacks were concluded, many of the ISIL fighters withdrew in good order into the desert, or blended into the local civilian population. The fighting on June 8th was crucial, as ISIL units infiltrated the city center and seized key government buildings, including the Federal Police headquarters, and the Mosul International Airport, which had served as a logistics hub for the US military in Iraq.[18] By June 11th, the vast majority of the ISF had withdrawn from Mosul or had surrendered to ISIL forces.

The complexities of these operations indicate that the ISIL military command intended to overwhelm the ISF by seizing control of urban areas simultaneously. The capture of Mosul represented an extraordinary military victory as it provided ISIL with a strategically vital intersection on key routes that link Iraq to both Syria and Turkey. During these operations, ISIL forces also seized large quantities of weapons, ammunition, and vehicles from the ISF. This equipment would later be used to support follow on military operations in both Iraq and Syria. Their summer campaign extended further east and south, seizing small communities, such as Salah ad-Din and Diyala, as well as the cities of Kirkuk and Tikrit. These advances enabled ISIL to link up with other units that were operating in Syria.

In an attempt to capitalize on their military success, as well as to develop a dedicated following, ISIL issued a series of media releases that marked the beginning of Ramadan. The most significant of these releases was a series of videos that were produced in five different languages announcing the establishment of the caliphate. The main spokesman of ISIL, Abu Muhammad al-Adnani, announced on June 29th that the caliphate would encompass territory running from the Iraqi province of Diyala in the east to the province of Alleppo in the west of Syria.[19] He also indicated that the official name for the group would now be referred to as the Islamic State (IS). On July 1st, al-Baghdadi released an audio statement praising the establishment of the caliphate. On the same day a video was entitled "The End of Sykes-Picot" that showed Islamic State forces removing a barrier that demarcated the Iraq-Syria border.

The establishment of the caliphate represented the final phase of the evolutionary design of the Islamic State. The development of this state makes the IS different from other terrorist or insurgent organizations. In order to exert control over the areas it now controls, the IS has established an elaborate system of governance that resembles a modern state. In most of the areas that fall under its control, the IS now provides judicial, religious, and social services, education programming, infrastructure projects, and regulations for a functional economy. In order to maintain the physical integrity of this developing state, the IS has formulated a military strategy which is primarily defensive in nature.

According to Jessica Lewis McFate, this strategy is not an indicator of organizational weakness, but rather a sign that the IS intends to expand its control over territory in both Iraq and Syria.[20] The IS's defensive operations will continue to include terrorist and classical guerrilla tactics, as well as efforts to expand into regions where it can establish depth and control of strategic ground. Their expansion and terrorist attacks in regions outside their control will enhance the defense of cities under their control. The regional networks and terrain that the IS currently controls will undoubtedly contribute toward it future survival. With territory, resources, and a population base to recruit and populate its depleted ranks, the IS can remain flexible and evade defeat.[21]

By the end of December 2014, it was estimated that the IS had close to 31,000 Islamic fighters within its ranks. After the capture of Raqqa and Mosul, the IS was able to accumulate vast quantities of munitions and modern weapons systems from the ISF, which included armored personnel carriers, main battle tanks, field artillery, as well as a variety of anti-aircraft guns and small arms. While the US-led air campaign in Iraq and Syria has slowed the pace of their momentum, their force capabilities and command and control construct remain largely intact.[22] It is estimated that the IS has lost nearly 6,000 fighters since the US-led air campaign began in August 2014.[23]

However, the Islamic State has exhibited a remarkable degree of resilience during this period. They have also proven to be adaptive and difficult to defeat decisively. In an asymmetrical conflict against nonstate entities, it is essentially impossible for a conventional force to achieve a decisive victory that denies an enemy the means and desire to continue fighting. As a hybrid organization, the IS has the ability to alter its war fighting structure to suit the environment that it is operating within, which will make defeating it significantly difficult. After a series of defeats suffered at the hands of the Syrian Kurdish forces at the beginning of October 2014 and continued pressure from US and allied warplanes, the IS has been able to resume its ground operations in both Syria and Iraq.

In May 2015, the IS forces seized al-Tanf, a key border crossing in Homs province from Syrian forces loyal to Assad. The capture of al-Tanf allows the IS forces to link up its forces in Iraq's Anbar province to their positions in eastern Syria more directly. This move paved the way for the IS to advance on Palmyra, which is an ancient desert city located in the center of Syria. Over the course of the last few months, the Islamic State forces have also begun to consolidate their positions in the Syrian provinces of Deir al-Zour, Raqqa, Hasakeh, Aleppo, Homs, and Hama.[24] Although these areas are not considered to be of significant strategic importance, they support the argument that the establishment of terrain through military conquest remains a major component of the IS's broader regional strategy. According to the Syrian Observatory for Human Rights, the IS now effectively controls more 50 percent of Syria.[25]

The Islamic State has also made significant military gains in Iraq, capturing the important city of Ramadi in Anbar province after weeks of intense fighting with the ISF in the beginning of May 2015. The IS has attempted to capture Ramadi as part of a broader strategy to invest all of Anbar. During this operation, the IS once again combined conventional mobile infantry units with terrorist cells to great effect. The IS initiated a series of SVBIEDs attacks against ISF and police units in order to dislodge them from their positions within the city and undermine the confidence of the civilian population. In an effort to divert ISF forces from Ramadi, the IS initiated a series of mobile diversionary attacks against the Baiji oil field. In addition to these operations, it also executed a number of terrorist attacks along other fronts. These operations had the effect of draining local reserves from the ISF and they succeeded in shifting the focus of the ISF away from Ramadi.

Towards the end of May 15th, IS forces seized the center of Ramadi and began to move down the Euphrates Valley in order to take the town of Habbaniya. The purpose of this operation was to link up with their forces in Fallujah, a city located next to Baghdad, which has been under their control for over a year. On conclusion of their military operations around Ramadi, the Islamic State effectively controlled one third of Iraq. However, the IS designs for Ramadi were part of a broader defensive strategy. This campaign was designed to consolidate terrain and prevent the ISF from concentrating its forces along a single front. The Islamic State was also in a position to regain the initiative in Iraq and drain valuable resources from a weakened ISF.[26]

Iraq also remains central to the IS's regional military strategy. The Islamic State's control of Mosul and Ramadi provide its forces with a strategic cauldron from which it can position and move forces freely between Iraq and Syria. The Jazeera Desert provides the IS forces with freedom of movement, allowing the military leadership to alternate forces between fronts and control large portions of Iraqi territory unimpeded.

Conclusion

The territorial expansion of the caliphate has been primarily achieved through a well-devised and synchronized military campaign. Through stages, the IS has evolved its capabilities and strategies that exploit the civil war in Syria and the sectarian divisions that continue to fester in Iraq. The Islamic State has exploited this environment by adopting a hybridized form of warfare. Although the disunity, inefficiency, and incompetence of the ISF unquestionably contributed to the success of the IS, they demonstrated a unique ability to coordinate and synchronize conventional forms of warfare with guerrilla tactics and terrorism. Through territorial conquests in Syria and Iraq, the IS has been able to translate military victories into considerable political achievements. The establishment of the caliphate has also significantly altered the security landscape of the Middle East as a whole. One of the main objectives of the IS is to elevate the level of instability in the region.

Over the course of the last year, the Islamic State has done much to undermine the state model that defines security within the international system. The legitimacy of the caliphate is based on the concept of controlled territory and effective governance. This is the basis of their political vision and legitimacy. In order to fulfill this political end-state, the IS must establish territory through military conquests, exert control through institutions, and defend the caliphate from foreign invaders. Although the IS has been defined as an Islamic jihadist movement, it is primarily a military actor, which has been devised and engineered to conquer territory and control populations.

NOTES

Introduction: Would Muhammad Join ISIS?

1. See the Associated Press story, "Monks Save Ancient Texts: Centuries-old Tomes Were Rushed to Kurdish City as Islamic State Militants Advanced," by Bram Janssen and Sameer Yacoub, published in the *Chronicle Herald* and other newspapers (April 4, 2015).
2. Posted on Reuters February 26, 2015, under the title, "With Sledgehammer, Islamic State Smashes Iraqi History," by Isabel Coles and Saif Hameed.
3. Media around the world carried the story on February 3, 2015, including posting the graphic video of the pilot being burned to death. One should see "ISIS Video Shows Jordanian Hostage Being Burned to Death," *The Guardian* (February 4, 2015).

Chapter 1: Americans Love Chick-fil-A; ISIS Loves Death

1. Bill Warner, *The Life of Mohammed: The Sira* (USA: CSPI, 2010), 2.
2. See helpful diagram here: http://cspipublishing.com/statistical/TrilogyStats/AmtTxtDevotedKafir.html.
3. Staff, "Islamic State group sets out first budget, worth $2bn," Al-Araby al-Jadeed, January 4, 2015. Available at: http://www.alaraby.co.uk/english/news/2015/1/4/islamic-state-group-sets-out-first-budget-worth-2bn.
4. Robert Windrem, "ISIS Is the World's Richest Terror Group, But Spending Money Fast," CNBC: NBS NEWS, March 20, 2015. Available at: http://www.cnbc.com/id/102522751.
5. Eric Schmitt, "In Battle to Defang ISIS, U.S. Targets Its Psychology," *New York Times,* December 29, 2014. Available at: http://www.nytimes.com /2014/12/29/us/politics/in-battle-to-defang-isis-us-targets-its-psychology-.html?_r=0.

Chapter 3: A Person of Interest

1. In recent years, some biblical scholars have proposed a sharp dichotomy between poor "peasants" in the countryside and the wealthy elite in the cities. Historians have rightly complained of this portrait, however, suggesting that a dubious Marxist understanding of society, economy, and history has been foisted on the world of Jesus. There is nothing in the ancient literature (e.g., Josephus) that suggests that farming and rural life in Galilee or elsewhere in Israel in the first century led to grinding poverty or that most in urban settings were somehow significantly better off.
2. We have probably found the tomb of the former and the burial box of the latter.

Chapter 4: The Dead Rise

1. Erica E. Phillips, 2014. "Zombie Studies Gain Ground on College Campuses: Students, Professors Study Culture of Living Dead," *Wall Street Journal*, March 3, 2014. Available at: http://www.wsj.com/articles/SB10001424052702304851104579361451951384512?cb=logged0.35197251243516803.
2. April 7, AD 33, is also an alterative date for the crucifixion of Jesus. For a more detailed analysis of the dating of Jesus's death and resurrection, see Robert H. Stein, *Jesus the Messiah: A Survey of the Life of Christ* (Downers Grove, Il; Leicester, England: InterVarsity Press, 1996), 39.
3. Daniel Alan Smith, *Revisiting the Empty Tomb: The Early History of Easter* (Minneapolis, MN: Fortress Press, 2010), 30. See also G. D. Fee, *The First Epistle to the Corinthians* (NICNT; Grand Rapids: Eerdmans, 1987), 722–729; J. A. Fitzmyer, *First Corinthians* (AB 32; New Haven and London: Yale University Press, 2009), 541: "The pre-Pauline proclamation is evident in its stereotypical formulation."
4. James D. G. Dunn, *Jesus Remembered. Christianity in the Making, Vol. 1* (Grand Rapids: Eerdmans, 2003), 855.
5. Ibid., 143.

Chapter 6: Hijacking Jesus

1. In the next chapter we shall review what the Qur'an says about the death of Jesus. We will again inquire into Muhammad's sources and evaluate their usefulness for historical research.

Chapter 7: The Qur'an vs. the Gospels

1. For translation and discussion, see F. F. Bruce, *Jesus and Christian Origins Outside the New Testament* (Grand Rapids: Eerdmans, 1974) 178–181.
2. The name *Ahmad* is from the same root as Muhammad. Qur'anic scholars believe that the reference to Ahmad in 61.6 is to Muhammad. The idea that Jesus foretold a successor may have been inspired by John 14:16, 26, and 16:7, where he spoke of the coming of a *Paraclete*, or Comforter.

Chapter 8: From California to the Caliphate

1. Jihadist News, "Islamic State Leader Abu Bakr al-Baghdadi Encourages Emigration, Worldwide Action," SITE Monitoring Service Jihadist Threat, June 29, 2014. Available at: https://news.siteintelgroup.com/Jihadist-News/islamic-state-leader-abu-bakr-al-baghdadi-encourages-emigration-worldwide-action.html.

2. Tom Kington, "Arab Wars Create 10,000 Refugees a Day." *The London Times,* May 7, 2015. Available at: http://www.thetimes.co.uk/tto/news/world/africa/article4432645.ece.
3. James Warren, Thomas Tracy, Larry McShane, "American who joined ISIS killed in Syria gunfight," *New York Daily News,* August 26, 2014. Available at: http://www.nydailynews.com/news/world/u-s-isis-member-douglas-mcauthur-mccain-s-family-knew-syria-trip-article-1.1917205.
4. Aisha Labi, "New Law in Britain Pushes Universities to Help Stanch the Flow of Islamic Fighters," *Chronicle of Higher Education* April 3, 2015, section A14.

Chapter 9: Trending Terrorism #ISIS

1. Jethro Mullen, "What is ISIS' appeal for young people?" CNN, February, 25, 2015. Available at: http://edition.cnn.com/2015/02/25/middleeast/isis-kids-propaganda/.
2. Jack Clotherty, Pierre Thomas, Jack Date and Mike Levine, "ISIS Propaganda Machine Is Sophisticated and Prolific, US Officials Say," ABC News: Nightline, May 7, 2015. Available at: http://abcnews.go.com/International/isis-propaganda-machine-sophisticated-prolific-us-officials/story?id=30888982.
3. J. M. Berger and Jonathon Morgan, "The ISIS Twitter Census: Defining and describing the population of ISIS supporters on Twitter," The Brookings Project on US Relations with the Islamic World Analysis Paper, *The Brookings Institution,* No. 20, March 2015. Available at: http://www.brookings.edu/~/media/research/files/papers/2015/03/isis-twitter-census-berger-morgan/isis_twitter_census_berger_morgan.pdf.
4. Council on Foreign Relations, "U.S. Intelligence in a Transforming World," CFR Events, March 13, 2015. Available at: http://www.cfr.org/intelligence/us-intelligence-transforming-world/p36271.
5. Clotherty, et al., 2015. "ISIS Propaganda Machine," ABC News.
6. Art Moore, "U.S. Military Bases Raise Threat Level Due To ISIS." WorldNetDaily, May, 8, 2015. Available at: http://www.wnd.com/2015/05/u-s-military-bases-raise-security-status-over-isis/.
7. US Department of State, Center for Strategic Counterterrorism Communications. Available at: http://www.state.gov/r/cscc/index.htm.
8. Schmitt, "In Battle to Defang ISIS, U.S. Targets Its Psychology."
9. Dina Temple-Raston, "How To Take The Internet Back From ISIS." *The New Yorker,* May, 7, 2015. Available at: http://www.newyorker.com/tech/elements/how-to-take-the-internet-back-from-isis.

Chapter 11: Reforming Islam, the Cult of Death

1. Evelyn Beatrice Hall, *The Friends of Voltaire* (London: G.P. Putnam's Son, 1907), 199.
2. Bill Warner, *Sharia Law for Non-Muslims* (USA: CSPI, 2010), 33.

Chapter 12: Crimes against Humanity

1. Aaron Blake, "Obama says the Islamic State 'is not Islamic.' Americans Disagree," *The Washington Post,* online September 11, 2014. In his speech Obama referenced ISIS as ISIL, which means "Islamic State of Iraq and the Levant." Some refer to ISIS as simply IS or "Islamic State." We acknowledge the excellent analysis offered in David Wood, "Will the Real Islam Please Stand Up?" *Christian Research Journal* 37.6 (2014) 8–15.
2. Wood, "Will the Real Islam Please Stand Up?" 8. Maajid Nawaz, founder of the Quilliam Foundation in London, is author of *Radical: My Journey out of Islamist Extremism* (Lanham, MD: Rowman & Littlefield Lyons Press, 2013).
3. M. M. Ali, *The Holy Qur'an: Arabic Text, English Translation and Commentary* (2nd ed., Columbus, OH: Lahore, 1951), 32 n. 107.
4. Ali, *The Holy Qur'an*, 260–261 n. 716.
5. Wood, "Will the Real Islam Please Stand Up?" 14–15.
6. A number of modern Islamic writers and apologists defend the seventy-two virgins tradition mostly through appeal to the Hadiths, Medieval commentaries, and various fatwas that have been issued on the topic.
7. The reference to the large breasts is omitted in translations of the Qur'an. See Ali, *The Holy Qur'an*, 1136 (where one may compare the English translation in the left-hand column with the Arabic text in the right-hand column). In the relevant footnote on page 1137 (n. 2649), Ali discusses the youthfulness of the companions but elects not to discuss their anatomy.

Conclusion: To Defend from Muhammad's Faith, Even If You Are Unable to Defend Yourself from His Sword

1. In the sixteenth century, Luther used Turks, Mohammadanism, Mohammedans, interchangeably, but primarily referred to "Muslims" as "Turks," collectively.
2. Martin Luther, *Luther's Works, Vol. 18: Minor Prophets I: Hosea-Malachi.* edited by Jaroslav Jan Pelikan, Hilton C. Oswald, and Helmut T. Lehmann (Saint Louis: Concordia Publishing House, 1999), 88.
3. Ibid., 59:281.
4. Ibid., 59:260.

5. Ibid., 60:294.
6. Ibid., 60:254.
7. Ibid., 254.
8. Ibid., 262.
9. Ibid., 261.

Special Report: The Islamic State as a Military Actor

1. Cole Bunzel, "From Paper State to Caliphate: The Ideology of the Islamic State," The Brookings Doha Center Analysis Paper, *The Brooking Institution,* No. 19, March 2015, 16.
2. Josef Schroefl and Stuart J. Kaufman, "Hybrid Actors, Tactical Variety: Rethinking Asymmetrical and Hybrid War," *Studies in Conflict and Terrorism,* 37, 2014, 868.
3. Bunzel, "From Paper State to Caliphate," 14.
4. "Islamic State," *Jane's World Insurgency and Terrorism*, December 11, 2014, 2.
5. Jessica D. Lewis, "Al-Qaeda in Iraq Resurgent: The Breaking the Walls Campaign, Part I," Middle East Security Report 14, *Institute for the Study of War*, September 2013, 7.
6. Brunzel, 17.
7. Ibid.
8. "ISI Claims 90—Man Raid in Haditha, Killing Dozens," *SITE Intelligence Group*, February 24, 2012.
9. Lewis, "Al-Qaeda in Iraq Resurgent," 10.
10. Suadad al-Salhy, "Al-Qaeda says it freed 500 inmates in Iraqi jail-break," *Reuters*, July 12, 2013.
11. Ibid., 11.
12. "Islamic State," *Jane's World Insurgency and Terrorism,* 3.
13. Bunzel, "From Paper State to Caliphate," 25.
14. Charles C. Caris and Samuel Reynolds, "ISIS Governance in Syria," Middle East Security Report 22, *Institute for the Study of War*, July 2014, 11.
15. Charles Lister, "Profiling the Islamic State," The Brookings Doha Center Analysis Paper, *The Brookings Institution*, No. 13, November 2014, 14.
16. Ibid., 14.
17. Patrick Cockburn, *The Rise of Islamic State: ISIS and the New Sunni Revolution*, (London: Verso Books, 2015), 11.
18. Liz Sly and Ahmed Ramadan, "Insurgents seize Iraqi city of Mosul as security forces flee," *The Washington Post*, June 10, 2014.
19. "Islamic State," *Jane's World Insurgency and Terrorism*, 17.

20. Jessica Lewis Mcfate, "The ISIS Defense in Iraq and Syria: Countering an Adaptive Enemy," Middle East Security Report 27, *Institute for the Study of War*, May 2015, 7.
21. Ibid., 9.
22. Lister, "Profiling the Islamic State," 17
23. Julian E. Barnes, "US, Iraq Prepare Offensive to Retake Mosul From Islamic State," *Wall Street Journal*, January 22, 2015.
24. "Islamic State seizes key Syria-Iraq border crossing," *BBC*, May 22, 2015.
25. "Islamic State carries out its motto 'lasting and exploding and seizes more than 50% of Syria,'" *Syrian Observatory for Human Rights*, May 21, 2015. Available at: https://www.syriahr.com/en/2015/05/islamic-state-carry-out-its-moto-staying-and-explading-and-seizes-more-than-50-of-syria/.
26. Patrick Martin, Genevieve Casagrande, and Jessica Lewis McFate, Lehmann, "Isis Captures Ramadi," *Institute for the Study of War*, May 18, 2015, http://understandingwar.org/backgrounder/isis-captures-ramadi.

SUGGESTED READING

Introduction

Thomas F. Madden, *The New Concise History of the Crusades* (Landham: Rowman & Littlefield, 2006).

Michael Coren, *Hatred: Islam's War on Christianity* (New York: Random House Signal, 2014). Brigitte Gabriel, *Because They Hate: A Survivor of Islamic Terror Warns America* (London: St. Martin's Griffin, 2008).

Brigitte Gabriel, *They Must Be Stopped: Why We Must Defeat Radical Islam and How We Can Do It* (London: St Martin's Griffin, 2010).

Jessica Stern, *Terror in the Name of God: Why Religious Militants Kill* (New York: Harper Perennial, 2004).

Jessica Stern and J. M. Berger, *ISIS: The State of Terror* (New York: Ecco, 2015).

Wafa Sultan, *A God Who Hates: The Courageous Woman Who Inflamed the Muslim World Speaks Out Against the Evils of Islam* (London: St Martin's Griffin, 2011).

Michael Weiss, *ISIS: Inside the Army of Terror* (New York: Simon & Schuster Regan Arts, 2015).

Chapter 1

Bill Warner, *The Life of Mohammed: The Sira* (USA: CSPI, 2010).

Staff, "Islamic State group sets out first budget, worth $2bn," Al-Araby al-Jadeed, January 4, 2015. Available at: http://www.alaraby.co.uk/english/news /2015/1/4/islamic-state-group-sets-out-first-budget-worth-2bn.

Robert Windrem, "ISIS Is the World's Richest Terror Group, But Spending Money Fast," CNBC: NBS NEWS, March 20, 2015. Available at: http://www.cnbc .com/id /102522751.

Eric Schmitt, "In Battle to Defang ISIS, U.S. Targets Its Psychology," *New York Times, December 29, 2014.* Available at: http://www.nytimes.com /2014/12/29/us/politics/in -battle-to-defang-isis-us-targets-its-psychology -.html?_r=0.

Chapter 2

John Bright, *A History of Israel* (Philadelphia: Westminster, 1959).

Leon Wood, *A Survey of Israel's History* (Grand Rapids: Zondervan, 1970).

Evan and Marie Blackmore, *Between Malachi and Jesus: Writings from the Maccabean and Roman Times* (Chillicothe, OH: DeWard, 2014).

John J. Collins and Adela Yarbro Collins, *King and Messiah as Son of God: Divine, Human, and Angelic Messianic Figures* (Grand Rapids: Eerdmans, 2009).

Craig A. Evans and Peter W. Flint (eds.), *Eschatology, Messianism, and the Dead Sea Scrolls* (Dead Sea Scrolls and Related Literature 1; Grand Rapids: Eerdmans, 1997).

Lester L. Grabbe, *Judaism from Cyrus to Hadrian.* Vol. 2: *The Roman Period* (Minneapolis: Fortress, 1992).

Chapter 3

Craig A. Evans, *Jesus and His World: The Archaeological Evidence* (London: SPCK; Louisville: Westminster John Knox Press, 2012).

Craig A. Evans, *Jesus and the Remains of His Day: Studies in Jesus and the Evidence of Material Culture* (Peabody, MA: Hendrickson, 2015), chapter 2.

Craig A. Evans, *Jesus and the Ossuaries: What Jewish Burial Practices Reveal about the Beginning of Christianity* (Waco, TX: Baylor University Press, 2003).

Chapter 4

Robert H. Stein, *Jesus the Messiah: A Survey of the Life of Christ* (Downers Grove, Il; Leicester, England: InterVarsity Press, 1996).

James D. G. Dunn, *Jesus Remembered. Christianity in the Making, Vol. 1* (Grand Rapids: Eerdmans, 2003).

Daniel Alan Smith, *Revisiting the Empty Tomb: The Early History of Easter* (Minneapolis, MN: Fortress Press, 2010).

Gordon D. Fee, *The First Epistle to the Corinthians* (NICNT; Grand Rapids: Eerdmans, 1987).

Erica E. Phillips, "Zombie Studies Gain Ground on College Campuses: Students, Professors Study Culture of Living Dead" *Wall Street Journal.*, March 3, 2014. Available at: http://www.wsj.com/articles/SB10001424052702304851104579361451951384512?cb=logged0.35197251243516803.

Chapter 5

Bruce D. Chilton, *Abraham's Curse: Child Sacrifice in the Legacies of the West* (New York: Doubleday, 2008).

Tarif Khalidi (ed.), *The Muslim Jesus: Sayings and Stories in Islamic Literature* (Cambridge, MA: Harvard University Press, 2001).

John Reeves (ed.), *Bible and Qur'ān: Essays in Scriptural Intertextuality* (Leiden: Brill, 2004).

Rodney Stark, *The Rise of Christianity: A Sociologist Reconsiders History* (Princeton: Princeton University Press, 1996).

Rodney Stark, *The Triumph of Christianity: How the Jesus Movement Became the World's Largest Religion* (New York: HarperOne, 2011).

Chapter 6

Andrew G. Bannister, *The Arabic Gospel of the Infancy: A Comparative Study* (CIS Foundational Papers in Islam 1; London: London School of Theology, 2004).

Andrew G. Bannister, *An Oral-Formulaic Study of the Qur'an* (Lanham and New York: Lexington Books, 2014).

James A. Beverley and Craig A. Evans, *Getting Jesus Right: How Muslims Get Jesus and Islam Wrong* (Pickering, ON: Castle Quay Books, 2015).

Chapter 7

Keith E. Small, *Holy Books Have a History: Textual Histories of the New Testament and the Qur'an* (Monument, CO: Avant, 2009).

Keith E. Small, *Textual Criticism and Qur'ān Manuscripts* (Lanham MD: Lexington Books, 2011).

James R. White, *What Every Christian Needs to Know about the Qur'an* (Bloomington, MN: Bethany House, 2013).

Chapter 8

Aisha Labi, "New Law in Britain Pushes Universities to Help Stanch the Flow of Islamic Fighters," *Chronicle of Higher Education*, April 3, 2015, section A14.

Jihadist News, "Islamic State Leader Abu Bakr al-Baghdadi Encourages Emigration, Worldwide Action," SITE Monitoring Service Jihadist Threat, June 29, 2014. Available at: https://news.siteintelgroup.com/Jihadist-News/islamic-state-leader-abu-bakr-al-baghdadi-encourages-emigration-worldwide-action.html.

Tom Kington, "Arab Wars Create 10,000 Refugees a Day," *The London Times,* May 7, 2015. Available at: http://www.thetimes.co.uk/tto/news/world/africa/article4432645.ece.

James Warren, Thomas Tracy, Larry McShane, "American who joined ISIS killed in Syria gunfight," *New York Daily News,* August 26, 2014. Available at: http://www.nydailynews.com/news/world/u-s-isis-member-douglas-mcauthur-mccain-s-family-knew-syria-trip-article-1.1917205.

Chapter 9

US Department of State, Center for Strategic Counterterrorism Communications. Available at: http://www.state.gov/r/cscc/index.htm.

J. M. Berger and Jonathon Morgan, "The ISIS Twitter Census: Defining and describing the population of ISIS supporters on Twitter." *The Brookings Institution.* Available at: http://www.brookings.edu/~/media/research/files/papers/2015/03/isis-twitter-census-berger-morgan/isis_twitter_census_berger_morgan.pdf.

Council on Foreign Relations, "U.S. Intelligence in a Transforming World," CFR Events, March 13, 2015. Available at: http://www.cfr.org/intelligence/us-intelligence-transforming-world/p36271.

Jethro Mullen, "What is ISIS' appeal for young people?" CNN, February, 25, 2015. Available at: http://edition.cnn.com/2015/02/25/middleeast/isis-kids-propaganda/.

Jack Clotherty, Pierre Thomas, Jack Date and Mike Levine, "ISIS Propaganda Machine Is Sophisticated and Prolific, US Officials Say," ABC News: Nightline, May 7, 2015. Available at: http://abcnews.go.com/International/isis-propaganda-machine-sophisticated-prolific-us-officials/story?id=30888982.

Art Moore, "U.S. Military Bases Raise Threat Level Due To ISIS" WorldNetDaily, May, 8, 2015. Available at: http://www.wnd.com/2015/05/u-s-military-bases-raise-security-status-over-isis/.

Dina Temple-Raston, "How To Take The Internet Back From ISIS," *The New Yorker*, May, 7, 2015. Available at: http://www.newyorker.com/tech/elements/how-to-take-the-internet-back-from-isis.

Chapter 10

Tom Holland, *In the Shadow of the Sword: The Birth of Islam and the Rise of the Global Arab Empire* (New York and London: Doubleday, 2012).

Chapter 11

Ayaan Hirsi Ali, *Heretic: Why Islam Needs a Reformation Now* (New York: Harper, 2015).

Ayaan Hirsi Ali, *Infidel* (New York: Atria, 2007).

Evelyn Beatrice Hall, *The Friends of Voltaire* (London: G.P. Putnam's Son, 1907).

Bill Warner, *Sharia Law for Non-Muslims* (USA: CSPI, 2010).

Chapter 12

Karen Armstrong, *Islam: A Short History* (New York: Modern Library, 2002).

David Cook, *Contemporary Muslim Apocalyptic Literature* (Syracuse: Syracuse University Press, 2005).

Jean-Pierre Filiu, *Apocalypse in Islam* (Los Angeles: University of California, 2011).

Robert Fisk, *The Great War for Civilisation: The Conquest for the Middle East* (New York: Alfred A. Knopf, 2008).

Tom Holland, *In the Shadow of the Sword: The Birth of Islam and the Rise of the Global Arab Empire* (New York and London: Doubleday, 2012).

Bernard Lewis, *The End of Modern History in the Middle East* (Stanford, CA: Hoover Institution Press, 2011).

Robert Spencer, *Not Peace but a Sword: The Great Chasm Between Christianity and Islam* (El Cajon, CA: Catholic Answers, 2013).

David Wood, "Will the Real Islam Please Stand Up?" *Christian Research Journal* 37.6 (2015), 8–15.

Guenter B. Risse, *Mending Bodies, Saving Souls: A History of Hospitals* (New York/Oxford: Oxford University Press, 1999).

Timothy S. Miller, *The Birth of the Hospital in the Byzantine Empire* (Baltimore/London: The Johns Hopkins University Press, 1985).

Conclusion

Jay Sekulow, Jordan Sekulow, and David French, *Rise of ISIS: A Threat We Can't Ignore* (New York: Howard Books, A Division of Simon & Schuster, Inc., 2014).

Benjamin Hall, *Inside ISIS: The Brutal Rise of a Terrorist Threa*t (New York: Hachette, 2015).

Johnnie Moore, *Defying ISIS: Preserving Christianity in the Place of Its Birth and in Your Own Backyard* (Nashville: Thomas Nelson, 2015).

Erick Stakelbeck, *ISIS Exposed: Beheadings, Slavery, and the Hellish Reality of Radical Islam* (Washington, DC: Regnery, 2015).

Martin Luther, *Luther's Works, Vol. 1-55; 58–60.* Edited by Jaroslav Jan Pelikan, Hilton C. Oswald, and Helmut T. Lehmann (Saint Louis: Concordia Publishing House, 1999–).

Tom Doyle, *Dreams and Visions: Is Jesus Awakening the Muslim World?* (Nashville: Thomas Nelson, 2012).

ACKNOWLEDGMENTS

Special Thanks to:

The Brookings Institute

The Congressional Research Service

The Soufan Group

The Center for the Study of Political Islam

The Munich Security Report 2015

Curtis Wallace, Law office of Curtis W. Wallace, P.C.

Houston Baptist University

Acadia Divinity College, Acadia University

Christian Thinkers Society

Jay Smith, Pfander Center for Apologetics

About Dr. Craig A. Evans

Dr. Craig A. Evans is the John Bisagno Distinguished Professor of Christian Origins at House Baptist University. He earned a doctorate in biblical studies at Claremont Graduate University in 1983 and a second doctorate at Karoli Gaspard Reformed University in Budapest in 2009. He is author or editor of more than fifty books, including *Jesus and His Contemporaries*, *Jesus in Context*, *Ancient Texts for New Testament Studies*, *Jesus and His World: The Archaeological Evidence*, *From Jesus to the Church*, and *God Speaks: What He Says and What He Means.*

Professor Evans has given lectures at Cambridge, Durham, Oxford, Yale, and other universities, colleges, seminaries, and museums, such as the Field Museum in Chicago and the Canadian Museum of Civilization in Ottawa. He also regularly lectures and gives talks at popular conferences and retreats on the Bible and archaeology, including the Biblical Archaeology Society summer sessions, as well as fall sessions at the annual Society of Biblical Literature meetings. He has lectured on the Dead Sea Scrolls, Jesus and archaeology, canonical and extra-canonical Gospels, and the controversial James Ossuary and has appeared several times on television news programs and documentaries.

Long-time residents of Canada, Professor Evans and his wife Ginny have recently moved to Houston, Texas. They have two grown daughters and a grandson.

About Dr. Jeremiah J. Johnston

Dr. Jeremiah J. Johnston is a New Testament scholar, teacher, apologist, and regular speaker on university campuses, churches, and popular venues. His passion is equipping Christians to give intellectually informed accounts of what they believe. Dr. Johnston completed his doctoral residency in Oxford in partnership with Oxford Centre for Christian Studies and received his PhD from Middlesex University (United Kingdom) with commendation. He has masters degrees from Acadia University (Canada) and Midwestern Baptist Theological Seminary (USA).

In addition to his popular publications, Dr. Johnston has distinguished himself with publications in scholarly, refereed journals and serials. These include entries in Oxford University Press and E.J. Brill reference works. He specializes in Christian origins, Jesus and the Gospels, and topics, especially apologetics, that are closely related to Jesus and the Gospels. These include the resurrection of Jesus, New Testament manuscripts (their number, nature, and reliability), extra-canonical Gospels, resurrection, and afterlife beliefs. He has presented academic papers at learned meetings and has examined ancient texts (papyri, codices, and the like) at renowned libraries, such as the Griffith Papyrology Room of Oxford University's Bodleian Library and the Beinicke Rare Book and Manuscript Library of Yale University. Dr. Johnston co-edits an academic series for Bloomsbury T&T Clark and is currently preparing a volume on Jesus in Cambridge University Press's distinguished *In Context* series. He has lectured throughout the United States, Canada, and the United Kingdom.

Dr. Johnston currently serves as the founder and president of Christian Thinkers Society, a 501(c)3 ministry dedicated to resident institute of Houston Baptist University where he also serves as Associate Professor in Early Christianity in the School of Christian Thought. Dr. Johnston resides in Houston, Texas with his wife and two children.

Christian Thinkers Society produces live events, media productions, conferences, and publications to *teach pastors and Christians to become thinkers and thinkers to become Christians.*

For more information, visit www.ChristianThinkers.com.

Connect with Jeremiah at:

Twitter: @JeremyJohnstonJ

Facebook: www.Facebook.com/ChristianThinkersSociety

Instagram: Jeremy_J_Johnston